WORLD WAR TWO

The GOOD THE BAD & the Ghastly
WORLD WAR TWO

TERRANCE DICKS

ILLUSTRATED BY KATHRYN LAMB

PICCADILLY • LONDON

Terrance Dicks lives in North London. A very well known author, he has written numerous books. Among his popular information humour books published by Piccadilly Press are *A Riot of Writers, A Riot of Irish Writers, Europe United, Uproar in the House,* and most recently, *A Right Royal History.*

Kathryn Lamb lives in Dorset. she has illustrated many humour and children's books including *Staying Cool, Surviving School* and *A Right Royal History* for Piccadilly Press.

Text copyright © Terrance Dicks, 1995
Illustration copyright © Kathryn Lamb,1995

Phototypeset from author's disk by Piccadilly Press.
Printed and bound in Great Britain by Hartnolls Limited, Bodmin, Cornwall for the publishers Piccadilly Press Ltd., 5 Castle Road, London NW1 8PR

A catalogue record for this book is available from the British Library

ISBN: 1 85340 301 6 (trade paperback)
1 85340 395 4 (hardback)

Jacket design and illustration Todd South

CONTENTS

INTRODUCTION

INDEX

INTRODUCTION

In the immortal words of E.C. Bentley:

'Geography is about maps
Biography is about chaps.'

But if biography is about chaps (and chapesses too of course),
so is history in a way.

There's an old saying, 'The hour brings forth the man.' In other
words, history produces the sort of man, or woman, needed by
the times. But there's no doubt that colourful and charismatic
personalities have their influence on history.

These exceptional types, The Good, The Bad and The Ghastly,
tend to pop up in times of war. The Second World
War produced a particularly good crop. Here are some of the
more striking.

Which category do they come in? You'll have to decide that for
yourself. We'll kick off with the biggest and baddest of all...

HITLER 1889-1945

ENTER ADOLF

Adolf Hitler was born in Braunau, Austria, in 1889, the son of a customs official. His father, Alois, was illegitimate and had originally taken his mother's family name, Schicklegruber. Later he changed his name from Schicklegruber to Hitler, the name of his father. (Lucky for Adolf – let's face it, 'Heil Schicklegruber!' just hasn't got the right ring to it.)

Like many famous, and infamous men, Adolf had an unhappy childhood. The main problem was his father. To the little town where he lived, Alois Hitler was a devoted civil servant. In private life he was a drunkard and a harsh, unloving father. A strict disciplinarian, he frequently beat his children, and his dogs, with a hippopotamus-hide whip. Hitler's older brother, Alois Jr, couldn't stand it and ran away from home when he was fourteen. With his big brother gone, Adolf got an even bigger share of the beatings. His mother Klara was devoted to him, and did her best to protect him from his father.

Not surprisingly, young Adolf grew up a wild, rebellious child. According to his sister Paula, he would challenge his father and got a sound thrashing every day.

CLASS REBEL

Like many rebels, young Adolf was something of a leader at school, organising his classmates in wild games of cowboys and Indians. Even though he was Austrian by birth, he loved reading about Germany beating France in the Franco-Prussian war in 1870. He showed a talent for art and spent much of his time in class sketching when he should have been working.

Hitler had already decided to be an artist or an architect, but Alois was determined to turn his rebellious son into a civil servant. When Adolf was eleven he was sent away to the Realschule, a kind of technical college in Linz. For a time, Adolf did well enough, but then his work started to slip. His teachers said he lacked self-discipline, and was 'cantankerous, wilful and arrogant' – and lazy as well. He hated being told off, and demanded that his class-mates obey him as their leader. He gradually became more and more solitary and more and more of a dreamer, convinced in some strange way, that a great destiny lay before him.

EXIT ALOIS

Alois died when Hitler was fourteen, which must have made life a lot easier for everyone, especially since he left a good civil service pension. Indulged by his adoring mother, Adolf left school without graduating, using ill-health as an excuse. For a while he just hung about at home, dreaming vague dreams of future greatness. He fell in love with a local girl, a beautiful blonde called Stephane, but was too shy to speak to her. Engaged to someone else, she didn't even know he existed. Hitler boasted about a romantic suicide pact, but it never came to anything (pity, really...).

VIENNA BOUND

Hitler had inherited a little money from his hated father and he decided to use it to go off to Vienna to become a great artist. But the Vienna Fine Arts Academy turned down his entry application, saying that his test drawings were unsatisfactory. (Just imagine, if Adolf had been a better artist, or the Academy a bit less strict, Hitler might have ended up a minor Austrian painter, instead of Dictator of Germany. We'd have had to put up with a few bad paintings, but the world would have been saved a lot of grief.)

On top of everything else, his adored mother became fatally ill. Hitler returned home for the last days of her illness. Although he had brothers and a sister, his mother was the only one in the family he'd ever been close to. After her death he went back to Vienna, more alone than ever.

HITLER MIGHT HAVE ENDED UP A MINOR AUSTRIAN PAINTER...

HIPPY HITLER

At this point Hitler entered his unhappy hippy period. Gradually his money ran out and he drifted around Vienna for the next few years, living in cheap lodgings and eventually ending up in the 'Mannheim', a cheap working men's hostel. He managed to earn the odd schilling by selling paintings and postcards to tourists. In his ankle-length overcoat and filthy black hat he looked very like a tramp. He started to take an interest in politics, attending meetings, reading pamphlets, and absorbing the nationalist – and anti-Jewish – sentiments common in Austria at the time. Sometimes he would deliver long ranting speeches to his fellow lodgers. In 'Mein Kampf' Hitler paints this as a time of high ideals and grinding poverty. 'Hunger was my constant companion,' he wrote. 'It never left me for a moment.'

In 1913, Adolf left the Mannheim to try his luck as an artist in Munich. Things were even tougher there than in Vienna and he had to sell paintings door-to-door to survive. When World War One broke out in 1914, he promptly volunteered to join the German Army – at least he'd be warm and fed.

CORPORAL ADOLF

Something of a loner, and regarded as a bit of a weirdo by the boys in the barrack-room, Adolf turned out to be a pretty good soldier, rising to the rank of lance-corporal. He was given the dangerous job of a runner, carrying messages up and down the front line. He was wounded twice and awarded the Iron Cross, First Class, for bravery in action. However, he never rose above the rank of corporal. Not only was he decidedly scruffy, he failed to show proper respect to his officers. His odd, solitary temperament held him back as well – it was felt he lacked talent for leadership! Near the end of the war, Hitler was caught in a gas attack, and was temporarily blinded.

PARTY TIME

When he recovered his sight, Hitler left hospital and returned to Munich. Like the rest of Germany, Munich was in a state of political chaos. Germany was still reeling under the shame of defeat, angrily resentful of the harsh terms imposed by the victorious Allies. Germany had lost all her overseas colonies, her armed forces were cut to a minimum, and the disputed Rhineland territory had gone back to France. In addition, the country's economy was crippled by 'Reparations', a massive fine for losing the war.

The hard-up Hitler had to take a job as a low-grade spy. The Army was anxious to keep an eye on all the new political parties. Special Agent Adolf was sent off to investigate the newly-formed National Socialist Workers Party – Nazi, for short. Its policies, if you could call them that, were a ragbag of ideas pinched from left and right – something for everybody, with a strong dose of anti-Jewish sentiments mixed in.

It was just a struggling, hard-up little political party, no different from dozens of others but Adolf decided it had possibilities. Instead of spying on it, he joined it. It was the turning point in his life – and a lot of other people's lives as well. Adolf's new friends included: a war-hero and fighter ace called Hermann Goering; Heinrich Himmler, a weedy ex-chicken farmer; Ribbentrop, the snobbish champagne salesman; and a ratty-looking little chap called Goebbels who had a gift for political propaganda. Like Hitler himself, they were nearly all misfits and failures.

ADOLF'S DESTINY

If you look at Adolf's life so far, it doesn't make a very impressive record. School rebel, failed artist ... Only his army service was even a modest success. Now he was on his way to ruling all Germany and much of Europe. How did he do it?

Unbalanced as he was, perhaps *because* he was so unbalanced, Adolf had one thing going for him – his conviction of his own greatness, his glorious destiny to lead Germany into a wonderful future. It had been burning deep inside him all his life. Now it had the strength of madness – a madness which could infect others. Throughout Hitler's career, all sorts of powerful and important people testified to the sheer hypnotic power of his personality. Fellow politicians, high-ranking army officers, wealthy industrialists – all were overwhelmed by the burning eyes, the rasping voice, and, above all, by Hitler's complete and utter certainty that he was right about absolutely everything!

HITLER GETS GOING

Adolf Hitler had found his role in life at last. In two years he had taken the Nazi Party over, ousting all his rivals to become its acknowledged leader.

One other talent was important in Hitler's career. He discovered an incredible gift for public speaking. One of Adolf's orations could whip any kind of crowd into a roaring frenzy. He started off slowly and hesitantly, and gradually lashed himself into total hysteria. He shouted and screamed and raved and ranted about all the enemies oppressing poor, unhappy Germany. He attacked the Allies and their peace treaty. Above all, he warned against the Jewish-Bolshevik conspiracy, a mysterious alliance of grasping capitalist financiers and fiendish communist revolutionaries who, according to Adolf, were to blame for all Germany's troubles.

AN INCREDIBLE GIFT FOR PUBLIC SPEAKING...

It was all absolute rubbish – and completely convincing while you were listening to it. In the years that followed, millions of hard-up, humiliated and unhappy Germans swallowed this poisonous nonsense entirely.

THE PATHETIC PUTSCH

The new party did so well that it got over-confident. In 1923 the Nazis tried a 'putsch', an attempt to seize power by force.

Hitler led a march on the Munich War Ministry. A police cordon blocked the way. When they refused to turn back the police fired a few shots and the bold revolutionaries ran like rabbits.

ADOLF IN CLINK

A normal politician would have given up by now, but Adolf's loony confidence transformed disaster into success. He turned his trial into a propaganda triumph, making more of his long ranting speeches from the dock. By the end of the trial, Adolf Hitler was a national figure – and a political force as well, feared by the German government. Sentenced to five years imprisonment, he ended up serving nine months – as a VIP prisoner in a comfortable cell in the Landsberg Fortress.

IN THE BOOK

Prison gave Hitler a chance to think over his mistakes. Trying to grab power by force had obviously been a bad move. From now on he'd stick to more or less legal means.

He also used the time to write 'Mein Kampf' – 'My Struggle' – his political testament. Long, rambling, and repetitious, this incredibly boring book spells out Hitler's plans to make Germany great again by attacking her enemies – Jews, communists, liberals, fiendish foreigners of every kind...

According to Adolf, what Germany needed was 'lebensraum' – 'living room'. In other words, more territory. All Hitler's plans for world domination are there in the book, but it was years before anyone took any notice.

THE ROAD TO POWER

Released from jail, Hitler, spent the next ten years rebuilding the party's fortunes. He already had one private army, the brown-shirted SA, or stormtroopers, led by Ernst Roehm. Now he set up another, the more exclusive black-uniformed SS, his own personal bodyguard.

Adolf's catch-all policies appealed to all classes of society. The bosses saw him as a defence against communists and trade unions. To the masses he promised jobs, prosperity and a restoration of Germany's former greatness.

ADOLF RULES

By 1933, the Nazis managed to get 44 per cent of the votes. By forming an alliance with the Nationalist Party Adolf gained a slender 52 per cent majority. He was in!

With amazing speed, the Nazis took over the country. New laws were passed, stripping the Reichstag of nearly all its powers, and giving them to the Chancellor. All other political parties were banned – the Nazi Party became the only party. Socialists, communists, liberals, trade unionists were beaten up, locked up, or murdered by Hitler's thugs. Based on Adolf's acceptance of loony notions about racial purity and the superiority of an imaginary blond and blue-eyed Aryan race, a relentless persecution of the Jews began. Gradually they were stripped of all their rights – and finally, of the right to live. The Holocaust, the deliberate massacre of six million Jews in the death camps, didn't come till later, but its seeds were there in Nazism from the beginning.

Hitler became the 'Fuehrer' ('Leader') and supreme Dictator of Germany. All army officers had to take an oath of allegiance, not to Germany, to Hitler himself.

THE GLORY YEARS

The years between 1933 and the early '40's were glory years for Adolf Hitler, the high point of his career. All Germany united in Hitler worship. Everyone joined the Nazi Party – it was the only way to get on. Even kids were dragooned into the Hitler Youth, a sort of Nazi version of the Boy Scouts.

HITLER YOUTH
(THE ONE ON THE RIGHT IS A PARTICULARLY WORRYING SPECIMEN)

Adolf addressed enormous party rallies at Nuremburg, political events that were stage-managed like rock concerts, or religious ceremonies, stage-managed by his image-maker Goebbels. There were cheering crowds, torchlight processions, and endless speeches.

ADOLF THE SEX SYMBOL

It wasn't just the men who worshipped the Fuehrer. Women wrote to Hitler from all over Germany, expressing their adoration, begging to meet him, offering to bear his child. Adolf had admirers all over the world. Unity Mitford, who came from an aristocratic English family, fell madly in love with him, came to live in Berlin to be near her idol, and committed suicide when war was declared.

Adolf, always a bit of a prude, was rather embarrassed by the whole thing. For an all-powerful dictator with any number of willing women at his feet, his life was relatively sleaze-free. (In 1931, before the Nazis came to power, there was an unsavoury scandal involving Adolf's attractive young niece Geli, in whom he took a rather more than uncle-like interest. Then Adolf made the acquaintance of another seventeen-year-old, a beautiful blonde called Eva Braun who worked in a photographic shop. Geli found out and committed suicide in a jealous rage. The whole thing was hurriedly hushed up.)

ADOLF THE SEX SYMBOL

Eva Braun became Hitler's mistress, and the relationship lasted for the rest of their lives. Hitler often talked about marrying her, and eventually did (see later).

PLAYING AWAY

With Germany in his iron grip, Adolf turned his attention abroad. He began by taking back the Rhineland. The French protested and threatened – but they didn't fight. Adolf went on to take over Austria. He got away with that too. When he moved to grab Czechoslovakia there was a storm of protest.

In 1938 there was an international conference in Munich. Hitler promised Britain's Prime Minister, Neville Chamberlain, not to gobble up any more of Europe – 'This is my final territorial demand'. Reassured, everyone went home happy, especially Adolf, who promptly started planning the conquest of Poland.

A GRAB TOO FAR

Hitler did a cynical deal with his old enemy Russia, agreeing to carve up a conquered Poland between them. He knew Poland had alliances with France and Britain, but he didn't expect them to do anything. He was astonished when his invasion of Poland in 1939 produced an ultimatum from Britain and France. 'Withdraw or it's war!' Hitler had gone too far to draw back now. It was war.

BLITZKRIEG

There was a feeling amongst the German General Staff that Germany had gone too far – but Adolf was as full of loony confidence as ever. Over-ruling his more cautious generals, he ordered a 'Blitzkrieg', a lightning-strike, through Belgium. Astonishingly, he got away with it again. With incredible speed Adolf's armies conquered Belgium, Holland, Denmark, Norway and France, leaving most of mainland Europe under Nazi rule.

It was a time of triumph, the high point of Hitler's promised 'Thousand Year Reich'. From now on Adolf knew he just couldn't lose. Ironically, it was at exactly this point that things started going wrong...

BRITANNIA AT BAY

Those pesky Brits were the first fly in Adolf's ointment. He'd chased their British Expeditionary Force right out of France. Now he started making plans for invasion. But the English Channel was wide, wet and stormy, and the German generals refused to cross it without control of the air. By now Hermann Goering was in charge of the 'Luftwaffe', the German air force.

'Leave it to me,' said fat Hermann, and Hitler did. The Battle of Britain was fought in the skies over England and the heroic young pilots of Britain's Royal Air Force won. Hitler got fed up with waiting for the promised command of the skies. 'Operation Sealion', the invasion of England, was postponed – indefinitely.

RUSSIAN ROULETTE

From Adolf's point of view it was a bad mistake – his first after years of unbroken success. He went on to make an even bigger one – a real whopper of an error.

Although Russia was technically still his ally, Adolf had always feared and hated the 'Bolshevik hordes', as he called them. In

June 1941 he launched a sudden, treacherous attack on Russia, confident that he could conquer it in six weeks. His army generals knew it was madness, but inflamed with his earlier successes, Hitler wouldn't listen. After all, he'd been right before, hadn't he? He was the Fuehrer. He was always right!

At first the invasion went well. German armies drove deep into Russian territory. The Russians simply pulled back – and back and back. But Adolf had underestimated the size of Russia and the determination of its people, and their leader, Joseph Stalin – a dictator as ruthlessly efficient as Hitler himself. Soon the German armies were over-stretched, with the deadly Russian winter on the way.

THE YANKS ARE COMING

Not long afterwards, Germany's Japanese allies also made a major mistake. Although still at peace with the USA, they decided to knock out the American Pacific Fleet with one devastating, unexpected blow. In December 1941 they attacked Pearl Harbour. The Americans were unprepared, the surprise attack was a success, and many American ships were destroyed in harbour. But the end result was to bring a very annoyed America into the war.

SEEDS OF DOOM

Suddenly Hitler was fighting not just Britain and her Empire but Russia and America, two angry giants with vast resources in materials and manpower. From this point he was doomed, although it took him quite some time to realise it.

Slowly but surely the tide of war turned against him. In 1942 the German Army, frozen and starving outside Stalingrad, was forced to surrender. The Allies defeated Hitler's armies in Africa. They invaded Sicily and started fighting their way up through Italy. And on D-day, June 6th 1944, a million Allied troops invaded the coast of occupied France. By now even Adolf's generals were turning against him. Snobbish, upper-class Prussians to a man, they'd never thought much of the Austrian corporal anyway. In July 1944 they did their best to blow him up. Unfortunately the bomb plot was unsuccessful.

ADOLF'S END

In 1945, with British, American and Russian troops advancing rapidly on Berlin, Adolf retreated to the 'Fuehrerbunker', an underground fortress beneath the Chancellery Gardens. Still refusing to accept reality, he moved non-existent army divisions about on the map, and declined to discuss surrender. Even now, it never occurred to him that he'd been wrong. The German people, he said, had proved unworthy of his genius.

On April 29th 1945 Hitler married his long-time girlfriend, Eva Braun. It was to be a very short honeymoon. Next day Hitler shot himself in his study, and Eva Braun took poison.

Did Hitler have his good side? He was devoted to his mother, kind to his Eva Braun, and very fond of Blondi, his pet Alsatian bitch. He was also a non-drinker, a non-smoker and a vegetarian – which just proves that clean living isn't everything it's cracked up to be.

HITLER WAS A VEGETARIAN

As we've seen, Adolf Hitler's success was short-lived. The 'Thousand Year Reich' lasted for just twelve years. In that time Hitler and his horrible henchmen plunged the world into war and caused an incredible amount of misery and suffering to their own countrymen, and to much of the world.

How Hitler achieved as much as he did is hard to explain although the unhappy state of the defeated Germany after World War One has a lot to do with it.

Perhaps the true answer lies in his astonishing personal charisma, fuelled as it was by the strength of madness. Paranoiacs have delusions of grandeur, of ruling the world. Really powerful paranoiacs manage, at least for a time, to make those dreams come true, altering reality to suit themselves.

Hitler's dreams became a nightmare for everyone.

CHAMBERLAIN 1869-1940

NICE NEVILLE

With Germany ruled by a power-mad dictator, determined to take over most of Europe, who did the British send in against him? A trusting old gent with a rolled umbrella and a funny hat!

Neville Chamberlain was really too nice to be a politician. So how did he get to be Prime Minister?

For a start, he was born into a political family. He was the son of Joseph Chamberlain, known as 'Brummagen Joe', a big man in Birmingham municipal politics who rose to be Lord Mayor, and later became a distinguished MP.

A TRUSTING OLD GENT WITH A ROLLED UMBRELLA AND A FUNNY HAT !

Neville was sent away to Rugby, the school where the well-known alternative to soccer was invented. Like most public schools in those days, it was a tough sort of place, keen on team games, cross country runs and cold showers.

Unfortunately, young Neville just wasn't the hearty type. Thin and nervous, and painfully shy, he didn't enjoy Rugby at all.

BAHAMAS AND BUSINESS

After a bad start in the Bahamas running an unsuccessful sisal plantation, Neville came home and embarked on a business career. Helped by his influential dad, he became a director of a firm which made brass and copper alloys, and of another making cabin bunks. He even took his first step in local politics. In 1911 he was elected to the council.

NEVILLE'S ROMANCE

Neville was forty by now, and seemed to be a born bachelor. But in that same year he met Anne de Vere Cole, the daughter of an army officer. After a whirlwind romance they were married.

Anne was the sister of Horace de Vere Cole, the famous practical joker who once dressed up as the Emperor of Ethiopia, sent the Navy a fake signal announcing the Emperor's arrival, and turned up to inspect a Royal Navy warship. (When the straitlaced Neville heard of the exploit he said sadly, 'Horace must be a bit mad!')

Anne seems to have shared some of her brother's high-spirits. Unlike Neville, who was dry and cautious, she was lively and emotional. She was something of a scatter-brain, and drove her orderly husband crazy by always being late. Her cheerful nature did a lot to liven up her rather stodgy husband. She probably did him a lot of good.

NEVILLE'S SUCCESS

Although he was still shy, and always found public speaking an ordeal, Neville was hard-working, well-organised, and a brilliant administrator. By 1914 he was an alderman, and a year later he became Lord Mayor of Birmingham. In 1918 he entered Parliament as MP for Birmingham.

For a respectable married man, with a totally sleaze-free life, Neville was surprisingly successful as a Conservative MP. His talent for hard work and efficient administration led to a rapid rise to Cabinet rank. He became Minister of Health in 1924 and Chancellor of the Exchequer in 1931. In 1937, at the age of 68, he became Prime Minister. It couldn't have happened to a nicer chap – or at a more unfortunate time.

CHAMBERLAIN AND APPEASEMENT

As Prime Minister, Neville Chamberlain is identified with 'Appeasement.' According to the dictionary, to *appease* means to pacify, to soothe, to satisfy someone's appetite. It's not a bad description of what Neville tried to do with Hitler.

Chamberlain was by no means the silly old fool that history sometimes makes him out to be. He had his reasons for appeasement. They all seemed to make sense at the time.

Like all his generation, Neville Chamberlain had lost friends and relatives in the horrors of the First World War – less than twenty years ago. Like nearly everyone else, he wanted to avoid war at almost any price.

An ex-Chancellor of the Exchequer, he was also worried by the cost of rearmament, which was endangering Britain's still-shaky recovery from depression, and hindering the domestic reforms close to Chamberlain's heart. He thought Britain needed schools and hospitals more than guns, tanks and planes.

Britain had an enormous empire to defend – and her military resources were already overstretched. If he could limit the arms bill by making a few diplomatic concessions, Chamberlain considered it well worth while. He described his policy as a 'double line'. Better relations with Germany – and limited re-armament at the same time.

FATAL INACTION

For all these reasons, Chamberlain took no action when Adolf invaded the Rhineland. He did nothing when Germany annexed Austria. However, when Hitler laid claim to the German-speaking Sudetenland, then part of Czechoslovakia, Chamberlain became concerned. He flew to Germany and had two meetings with Hitler, one at Berchtesgarden and one in Godesberg, trying, without success, to persuade Hitler not to invade. At a third meeting in Munich between Hitler, Mussolini, Chamberlain and French Prime Minister Daladier, Hitler modified his demands a little. Chamberlain said they were 'acceptable' and Hitler promised no more territorial demands. (The Czechs, whose country was being carved up, weren't consulted – they weren't even at the meeting.)

Peace with honour – not!

PEACE WITH HONOUR — NOT !

On September 30th 1938 Chamberlain flew home. At the airport he waved a piece of paper which he said, 'bears Herr Hitler's signature and my own.' The Munich Agreement, said Chamberlain, meant 'Peace with honour.' Some hopes! (Asked why he bothered to sign a treaty he had no intention of keeping Hitler said, 'Well, he seemed such a nice old gentleman, I thought I'd give him my autograph as a souvenir!')

Chamberlain may have been too trusting, but he was neither a coward nor a fool. When Hitler started moving in on Poland, Chamberlain decided that enough was enough. He guaranteed Poland's independence, and joined with France to issue an ultimatum – get out of Poland, or face war. Hitler chose war. Even though Chamberlain stood up to Adolf in the end, it was all too late.

EXIT NEVILLE

Chamberlain tried to put a brave face on it. 'Hitler has missed the bus,' he said. But most people thought Adolf was driving the bus – straight at them!

Chamberlain had lost the confidence of Parliament. When the beginning of the war went badly for Britain, with early defeats in Norway and France, Neville Chamberlain got the blame. He was attacked by his own party and defeated in Parliament. A fellow Conservative MP, Leo Amery, quoted Oliver Cromwell's speech to him: 'Depart, I say, and let us have done. In the name of God, go!' Chamberlain went. He resigned as Prime Minister, on the 10th May 1939 and Winston Churchill took over. Neville Chamberlain stayed on as a member of the War Cabinet, and as leader of the Conservative Party. Worn out by all his responsibilities, he died, less than a year later, in November 1940.

SUMMING UP

The historian AJP Taylor said Neville Chamberlain was 'a meticulous housemaid, great at tidying up...' Because of his well-intentioned policy of appeasement, Chamberlain has been blamed for letting us drift into war. But it's all too easy to condemn him, with the benefit of hindsight. If he'd stood up to Hitler earlier, things might have been different. But to be fair, hardly anyone at the time wanted another war – except Adolf, of course...

CHAMBERLAIN WAS 'A METICULOUS HOUSEMAID, GREAT AT
TIDYING UP...'

A.J.P. TAYLOR

Sad to say, by trying so hard to avoid another war, decent old Neville Chamberlain did more than most to bring it about.

CHURCHILL 1874–1965

WONDERFUL WINSTON

So fuddy-duddy old Neville Chamberlain was out at last. Who did the House of Commons choose to replace him? Some brilliant young politician with new ideas for winning the war?

Not a bit of it!

They chose a hard-drinking, cigar-smoking, upper-class renegade of sixty-six who'd changed parties twice, was regarded as a has-been, and who'd been in the political wilderness for years. (Just as well they did, or we'd all be speaking German.)

EARLY ARRIVAL

Winston Leonard Spencer Churchill was born in 1874 at Blenheim Palace, the magnificent home given by the nation to his great ancestor, John Churchill, Duke of Marlborough. Not that his family actually lived there. Winston's parents, Lord Randolph Churchill and his American wife Jenny, were attending a ball when Winston arrived unexpectedly early. (Some people said Jenny did it on purpose, just to get her baby born in the palace. She'd certainly insisted on attending the ball, despite being very pregnant.)

Winston had the typical upper-class upbringing of the time, seeing more of his nanny and the other servants than of his actual parents. Nevertheless, he adored his lively American mother. He found his father remote, and difficult to get to know.

CHURCHILL WAS BORN IN 1874 AT BLENHEIM PALACE

YOUNG WINSTON

In due course Winston was sent away to Harrow, where he had a pretty undistinguished career. He liked English, but Latin and mathematics were beyond him. It took him three tries to get into the Royal Military Academy at Sandhurst. He managed it at last, and found that he enjoyed Sandhurst much more than Harrow. He loved riding, 'No hour of life is lost that is spent in the saddle', and became a keen polo player.

FIGHTER AND WRITER

Winston was eventually commissioned into a cavalry regiment, the Fourth Hussars. He served in India and later in the Sudan, where he took part in a traditional cavalry charge.

In between his military duties, and frequent games of polo,

Winston set about educating himself. He was beginning to realise how little he'd actually learned at Harrow. He developed a useful side-line as a war correspondent and even wrote a book about soldiering on the North-West frontier. The book, 'The Malakand Field Force' was a great success. Winston was delighted. 'I had never been praised before,' he wrote, rather touchingly. 'The only comments which had ever been made upon my work at school had been "Indifferent", "Untidy", "Slovenly", "Bad", and "Very Bad!" '

He went on to write a second book, 'The River War' about the campaign in the Sudan.

HOME AND AWAY

Encouraged by his success, Winston decided to go into politics. Resigning his commission, he went home to England and stood for Parliament, fighting a by-election in Oldham. He lost, and went back to London feeling, he said, as flat as a bottle of champagne left open overnight. But Winston soon bounced back. The Boer War had just begun, and Winston went off to cover it as a war correspondent.

He hadn't been in South Africa very long when he was captured by the Boers when they attacked an armoured train. He was taken to Pretoria and imprisoned in a school with sixty other officers.

PRISONER OF WAR

At first Winston was in despair. 'Prisoner of War!' he told himself, 'you are in the power of your enemy...' But it wasn't in Winston's nature to be downhearted for long. He began planning escape. Hiding in a lavatory, he waited till the sentries' backs were turned and climbed out of the window and over the garden wall. He was free, but he was still three hundred miles from safety. Making his way to the nearby railway line he smuggled himself on a goods train, hiding amongst empty coal-sacks.

It was the beginning of a long and adventurous journey. Helped by English sympathisers who hid him in a coal mine and smuggled him on to another goods train, Winston eventually reached Lorenco Marques in Portuguese territory. He staggered up to the British Consulate, and was sent back to Durban by boat. News of his escape had spread, and cheering crowds awaited him on the quayside.

RETURNING HERO

Winston admitted later that being captured by the Boers was the best thing that ever happened to him. His daring escape had made him a public hero.

He returned to England, stood for Parliament in the general election of 1900, and became MP for Oldham.

In 1908 he met his beloved Clementine, and began a typically Churchillian whirlwind courtship. Clementine, Clemmie for short, was a beautiful and aristocratic young girl with a keen interest in the new women's liberation movement. (They didn't even have the vote in those days.) She was strong-minded enough to manage Winston, and tactful enough not to let it show. They married that same year and, as Churchill said, 'lived happily ever after.'

CHURCHILL AND CLEMENTINE LIVED
HAPPILY EVER AFTER.

A LIFE IN POLITICS

From now on, politics were to be Winston Churchill's life – but there were plenty of ups and downs ahead. In 1904, dissatisfied with the leadership of the Conservative Party, Winston defected to the Liberals, the other main party in those days. In 1906 he joined the Liberal Government as Under-secretary for the colonies. In the First World War he became First Lord of the Admiralty.

IN AND OUT – AND IN AGAIN

Winston's war career was to be a stormy one. He backed a daring plan to attack Turkey, Germany's ally. Whatever the merits of the plan, the Gallipoli campaign was inefficiently carried out, and ended up as a total disaster. It wasn't all Churchill's fault by any means, but he accepted responsibility. In 1915 he resigned from the Government and re-joined the Army. Soon afterwards, as Major Churchill of the Oxfordshire Yeomanry, Winston sailed for France.

Middle-aged as he was, he served through the thick of the fighting and was promoted to lieutenant-colonel. He nearly became a general, but political enemies back home blocked his promotion. A courageous and popular commanding officer, Winston enjoyed the danger and excitement of war. 'War is a game to be played with a smiling face,' he said.

At the same time, Churchill knew he could be far more use in Parliament. In 1917 he returned as Minister of Munitions, pouring all his energy into getting shells and ammunition to the troops.

WINSTON BETWEEN THE WARS

After the war, Churchill became disillusioned with the Liberals and drifted back to the Conservatives again. (Charged with political treachery he said loftily, 'Anyone can rat – but it takes real talent to re-rat!')

Churchill lost his seat in the 1922 elections but by 1925 he was back in Parliament, being offered a cabinet post by Conservative Prime Minister, Stanley Baldwin.

Winston describes the occasion in his own inimitable style:

'When he said, "Will you be Chancellor of the Exchequer?" I was astonished. I should have liked to have answered, "Will a bloody duck swim?" – but as it was an important and formal occasion I replied, "I shall be delighted to serve you in this splendid office.'"

Despite this promotion, things went badly for Winston. His reckless and outspoken nature didn't fit too well into the stuffy system of the Conservative Party. In 1931, with Ramsey MacDonald's Labour Government in power, Churchill resigned from the Conservative Shadow Cabinet and returned to the back benches.

WINSTON IN THE WILDERNESS

The thirties were a low-point in Winston's political life. He was out of office, distrusted by Conservatives, Liberals and Labour alike. Many thought he was a has-been, his career as good as over. In fact in 1932 Lady Astor, Britain's first woman MP visited Russia and told Stalin 'Churchill is finished!' (Mind you, they'd never got on. 'Winston, if I were married to you I'd put poison in your coffee,' Nancy once said, to which Winston replied, 'Nancy, if you were my wife, I'd drink it.') Churchill himself said in 1938, 'My career is a failure, it is finished. There is nothing more to offer.'

In the appeasing thirties, Winston was one of the few MPs to point out the danger represented by the ambitions of the fascist dictators, Hitler and Mussolini. He was appalled by the sell-out at Munich. 'We have sustained a total and unmitigated defeat,' he told Parliament. 'And do not suppose that this is the end. It is only the beginning.'

Winston was right – but nobody wanted to know.

'WINSTON'S BACK!'

The outbreak of war revitalised Churchill's career. In 1939 he was appointed First Sea Lord. A signal went out to the Navy – 'Winston's back!'

A year later, with the war going badly for Britain, Winston Churchill became Prime Minister of a coalition Government.

His speeches inspired the whole country. 'I would say to the house, as I said to those who joined the Government, I have nothing to offer but blood, toil, tears and sweat.'

He found another immortal phrase for the young pilots who saved England from invasion in the Battle of Britain: 'Never in the field of human conflict was so much owed by so many to so few.' And in his most famous speech of all he promised, 'We shall fight on the beaches...we shall fight in the fields and in the streets, we shall fight in the hills. We shall never surrender.'

HOLDING ON

Churchill's main achievement was to persuade the British people to hold on at a time when things looked hopeless.

When Hitler threatened to 'wring Britain's neck like a chicken's', Churchill rumbled, 'Some chicken! Some neck!'

He developed a valuable friendship with America's President, Roosevelt, who was sympathetic to Britain's cause. When the Japanese attack on Pearl Harbour brought America into the war the tide began to turn.

'SOME CHICKEN! SOME NECK!'

THE ROAD TO VICTORY

There was a long, hard struggle ahead, but gradually the balance of the war began tipping against Adolf and his allies.

In his role of Minister of Defence, Churchill presided over Britain's part in the struggle drinking champagne, smoking cigars, and working, it seemed to his exhausted staff, around the clock. (Winston could do this because he was a great believer in the mid-day siesta. An hour's nap after lunch and he was ready to go on all night.)

... DRINKING CHAMPAGNE, SMOKING CIGARS
AND WORKING, IT SEEMED TO HIS
EXHAUSTED STAFF, AROUND THE CLOCK.

He interfered everywhere, inspiring and often aggravating, the rest of his Government. He quarrelled furiously with his generals, and didn't hesitate to sack them if he wasn't happy with their performance. At the same time he was aware of his own tendency to rashness. 'Remember, I have the medals of Antwerp, Gallipoli, Norway and elsewhere pinned to my chest,' he once said, referring not to past victories, but to past disasters. Unlike his opponent Adolf, Winston knew he could be wrong.

Roosevelt admired him, but was always a bit wary of him. 'Winston has one hundred ideas every day, and one of them is almost sure to be right!'

UNEASY ALLIES

Winston Churchill also did great work in providing a link between America and Russia, those two unlikely allies. (Asked how he could bear to make an ally of his old enemy, communist Russia, Churchill said, 'If Hitler were to launch an attack on Hell itself, I would at least contrive to make a favourable reference to the devil in the House of Commons.')

THE REWARDS OF VICTORY

Peace came at last in 1945, with Germany crushed by the armies of the Allies, and Japan terrified into surrender by the dropping of two atomic bombs. The Americans and Russians settled down to fight the Cold War.

In Britain, the wartime coalition government was dissolved, and there was a general election. Of course it was quite clear who would win. After all, the Conservatives were led by the well-beloved Winston Churchill, the saviour of his country. The result was a landslide — for the other side. Astonishingly, the British people, swept up by a desire for social change, had decided that their great wartime leader wasn't the man they needed in peacetime.

TWILIGHT YEARS

Taken aback, but philosophical, Winston became Leader of the Opposition. (As he and Clemmie left Number Ten Downing Street, Winston muttered, 'We'll be back!')

And so they were. Labour's brave new world turned out to be a bit of a disappointment, and Winston became Prime Minister again in 1951, at the age of 77. He was getting a bit deaf by now, and occasionally confused the two world wars, but the Tories were reluctant to lose their main electoral asset. Old age caught up even with Winston at the end and he retired in 1955, at the age of 81. He lived in contented retirement for another ten years, pursuing his hobby of painting.

Winston Churchill died, aged 91, in 1965. He was given the biggest state funeral since the death of the Duke of Wellington.

THE HAPPY WARRIOR

Winston Churchill lived a full and mainly enjoyable life. He loved good food, strong drink – 'I have taken more out of alcohol than alcohol has taken out of me!' – big cigars and an afternoon nap.

Brash and bouncy when young, a bit of a bossy-boots when older, he seemed to have been left over from a tougher, more vigorous age, just to be there when we needed him.

In a surprisingly modest speech on his eightieth birthday Winston Churchill said, 'I have never accepted what many people have kindly said, namely that I inspired the nation. It was the nation and the races dwelling all around the globe that had the lion's heart. I had the luck to be called upon to give the roar.'

Some lion. Some roar...

ROOSEVELT 1882-1945

FDR

For a future President of the world's greatest democracy, Franklin Delano Roosevelt — FDR for short — had a very upper-class upbringing.

He was born into one of America's oldest families, the adored only child of a millionaire businessman, and educated at Groton, the American equivalent of a top English public school. (He arrived in his father's private railway carriage!)

From Groton he went on to Harvard, where he lived the life of a rich and fashionable student, filling his time with dinners, dances and parties. Franklin seemed typical of his class, well-dressed, cheerful and high-spirited, with the confidence and easy charm of a rich young man who'd always had whatever he wanted.

FRANKLIN AND ELEANOR

In 1903 he showed his first spark of independence. He announced his intention of marrying his distant cousin, Eleanor Roosevelt. His parents were amazed and none too pleased, feeling that at twenty-two he was too young to marry. Besides, Eleanor seemed almost his opposite, shy and rather plain, strong-willed and formidably intellectual. But Franklin had fallen hard. Gently, but firmly, he brushed aside family opposition and he and Eleanor were married in 1905.

LAW AND POLITICS

Franklin entered Harvard Law School, passing his bar exams in 1907. After that he entered a famous Wall Street law firm, but he had no intention of sticking with the law. Franklin wanted to follow in the footsteps of his famous cousin, Teddy Roosevelt, whose brilliant career in politics had ended in the White House.

FRANKLIN'S CAMPAIGN

In 1910 the local Democratic Party offered him the chance to run for the New York State Senate – in a solidly Republican district! Everyone knew young Franklin couldn't win. But he came from a well-known local family, and he was rich enough to pay for his own campaign.

Franklin plunged into politics with enthusiasm. Renting the only car for miles around, he drove all over his district, shaking hands and making speeches. His hard work paid off. To everyone's astonishment he won, defeating his Republican opponent by a thousand votes.

F.D.R. IN HIS CAR (A MAN WHO WOULD GO FAR — BUT NOT IN THAT CAR!)

RISING STAR

Franklin's rise was rapid after that. Tall, handsome, charming, and above all, rich, he was the perfect politician. Despite his over-privileged background he was tough and hardworking as well. By 1914 he was Assistant-secretary to the Navy, doing good work in that post throughout the First World War.

In 1920 he ran for Vice-President, and lost. Franklin wasn't downhearted: 'The moment of defeat,' he said, 'is the best time to plan for future victories.' But an unexpected enemy was waiting – one that even Franklin Roosevelt would find it hard to defeat.

FRANKLIN WAS WELL-DRESSED, CHEERFUL
AND HIGH-SPIRITED ...

POLIO STRIKES

One summer holiday afternoon in 1921, Franklin felt unusually tired after a swim with his children. Next morning when he woke up, one leg was numb. A specialist was sent for and it was discovered that Roosevelt was suffering from poliomyelitis – commonly called polio. The disease was also known as infantile paralysis, since it often attacked children. Today polio can be prevented by a vaccine, but in 1921 there was no known cure. Some victims became completely paralysed. Many died.

Roosevelt was severely ill for many weeks. He was taken to hospital where he slowly recovered. His life was no longer in danger, but both legs were paralysed.

FRANKLIN FIGHTS BACK

Roosevelt fought hard against his illness, refusing to be defeated by his handicaps. He was fitted with steel and leather leg-braces. After a long and agonising struggle, he learned to walk with the aid of crutches. By 1924 he was ready to return to politics.

ROOSEVELT'S COMEBACK

On June 26th he struggled to the rostrum in Madison Square Garden in New York and made a speech supporting the presidential nomination of a politician called Al Smith. Roosevelt's speech brought the crowd to its feet, cheering. Smith lost the nomination – but for Franklin Roosevelt it was a triumphant comeback. The Roosevelt who returned to politics wasn't the easy-going golden-boy of a few years earlier. Suffering had matured him, bringing wisdom and compassion.

ROOSEVELT GOES ON

By 1928 Roosevelt was campaigning for the governorship of New York State. He travelled all over the state, meeting the voters, making speeches and standing up in the back of an open car. He won, by the narrowest of margins.

When Roosevelt took office in 1929, America was rich and prosperous. Two years later, it was in the grip of depression.

ROOSEVELT AND THE GREAT DEPRESSION

The collapse of the stock market left America in economic chaos. Banks went bust, businesses closed down, stockbrokers jumped from skyscrapers. Millions of jobs just disappeared. Roosevelt set up special agencies to provide work, shelter, food and clothing for the needy. Under his leadership, New York State was the first state in America to take direct action to counter the effects of the Great Depression.

1932 was presidential election year. Thanks to his depression-fighting achievements, Roosevelt became a leading candidate, promising the people a 'New Deal'. When election time came round, Roosevelt won by a landslide.

PRESIDENT FDR

Once in office, Roosevelt continued his depression-fighting work, this time on a national scale. Hundreds of New Deal agencies were set up to provide jobs, food and shelter.

Not everyone approved. Roosevelt's most bitter opponents came from his own class – the rich and powerful. They resented his radical policies, and his higher taxes. In the 1936 election most of the newspapers in the country opposed Roosevelt. But the people still trusted him, and he won by another landslide.

FRANKLIN AND THE DICTATORS

Hitler came to power in 1933, during Roosevelt's first presidency. FDR had little time for Nazism. He was appalled by the suppression of civil liberties and horrified by the growing persecution of the Jews. He ordered the State Department to bend immigration rules so that more and more refugees could come to America from Germany and Austria. Roosevelt knew Hitler was evil and should be opposed, but his hands were tied.

ISOLATIONIST AMERICA

America had got mixed up in one European war in 1916. Most Americans, understandably enough, had no desire to repeat the experience. (Public opinion polls in 1939 showed that while 82 per cent of Americans wanted the British and their allies to win, 99 per cent were against US involvement in a foreign war.)

'Isolationism', as it was called, became a powerful political movement, supported by leading Democrats and Republicans alike. Millionaire newspaper tycoon, William Randolph Hearst, and aviation hero, Charles Lindbergh, were amongst its leaders. Joseph Kennedy, father of future President John F. Kennedy, was American Ambassador in London at the beginning of the war. 'This war is not our war,' he said. 'Britain is not fighting our battle.'

Roosevelt himself was sympathetic to the Allied cause. However, like any politician, he had to take notice of public opinion – especially with a presidential election coming up.

FRANKLIN'S CUNNING PLAN

Roosevelt's critics accused him of always following public opinion. The humorist, H.L.Mencken, said that if Roosevelt became convinced there were votes in cannibalism, he'd start fattening a missionary in the White House backyard. But Roosevelt was determined to help Britain. He swung public opinion towards the British cause in a series of radio broadcasts known as his 'fireside chats'. In 1939, soon after Hitler invaded Poland, he persuaded Congress to repeal the Neutrality Act. Now Britain could buy arms from America, so long as she paid cash, and took the arms away in her own ships. Bypassing Congress, Roosevelt made a 'Destroyers-for-Bases' deal with Churchill, swapping fifty old American destroyers for British bases in the Caribbean.

LEND-LEASE

After his re-election in 1940, Roosevelt was in a stronger position – which was more than could be said for poor old Britain. She desperately needed more war materials from America, but by now she was just too broke to pay for them.

Early in 1941, after long and difficult debate, Roosevelt persuaded Congress to pass the Lend-Lease Act. This allowed the President to 'lend or lease' Britain the war materials she needed, to be paid for after the war.

AMERICA AT WAR

Japan's treacherous attack on Pearl Harbour in December 1941 – Roosevelt called it a 'Day of Infamy' – brought America into the war, finally putting paid to the Isolationist lobby.

Roosevelt's responsibilities were greater than ever. As President he was automatically Commander in Chief of the American forces – although, unlike the ever-interfering Churchill, Roosevelt tended to choose his commanders and let them get on with the job. He also had to supervise America's mobilisation, both military and industrial – an immensely complex task.

ROOSEVELT THE REFEREE

Roosevelt also had to hold the balance between Churchill and Stalin, two strong leaders with their own very different ideas about the shape of the world after the war. Roosevelt got on surprisingly well with the Russian leader. He felt that it was Stalin's exclusion from world affairs before the war that had made him so suspicious and paranoid. He hoped to bring Russia into the 'family of nations.'

ROOSEVELT HAD TO HOLD THE BALANCE BETWEEN CHURCHILL
AND STALIN...

THE END OF FDR

Roosevelt saw the final defeat of Hitler – the defeat he had done so much to bring about. But he didn't live long enough to see his hopes of friendship with Russia dashed by the descent of what Winston Churchill called an Iron Curtain across Europe, followed by the bitter struggle of the Cold War. Franklin Roosevelt died of a massive cerebral haemorrhage in 1945, not long after being re-elected for an unprecedented fourth term.

Roosevelt wore himself out in the service of his country, and of the world. Brought up in luxury, he became a crusader for the poor and miserable. Crippled by polio, he bore the illness without complaint. So well did he disguise his handicap that few Americans even realised that he was crippled.

Lyndon B. Johnson, a later President, summed up the character of Franklin Delano Roosevelt, the man who carried so many burdens for his country and for the world: 'He was the only man I ever knew – anywhere – who was never afraid. God, how he could take it for us all.'

STALIN 1879–1953

THE MAN OF STEEL

The man who did much to scupper Roosevelt's hopes of post-war Russian-American friendship was Joseph Stalin. It wasn't his real name of course; that was the romantic revolutionary name chosen by a certain Joseph Vissarionovitch Djugashvili.

STALIN MEANS MAN OF STEEL

Stalin was born in Gori, Georgia, in 1879, with Russia still under the Czars. He was his mother's fourth child, the only one so far to survive. (A sister was born later.) His father, Vissarion, was a cobbler. The business didn't bring in a living wage, and Stalin's mother supported the family by taking in washing. Embittered by failure, Vissarion took to vodka. He also took out his anger on his wife and son. According to one of Stalin's childhood friends, 'Undeserved and frightful beatings made the boy as grim and savage as his father.' (It's interesting to note the similarities with the childhood of Adolf Hitler. Maybe regular beatings are a recipe for producing dictators.)

BRIGHT BUT POOR

Childhood smallpox gave Stalin his pockmarked face, and an ulcer on his arm left him unable to bend it at the elbow. Despite these early setbacks, young Joe grew up a tough and wiry kid, clearly one of nature's survivors. At the little village school he was the poorest and the cleverest kid there. He whizzed through his lessons almost without effort, and took pride in being brighter than the better-off kids in his class.

STUDENT STALIN

In those days, the church was almost the only way for poor but clever children to get on. Stalin's mother decided that he should be a priest. He was sent to a seminary (a priest's training college) in Tiflis. It was a grim, barracks-like building where students slept thirty to a dormitory. Food was short, conditions were primitive and discipline was enforced by stern monks. Students spent their days in theology lectures and in endless prayer. Only books authorised by the monks could be read and anything political was strictly forbidden.

THE YOUNG STALIN WINS ANOTHER ARGUMENT AT THE STUDENT DEBATING SOCIETY.

STUDENT REVOLT

Inevitably, the students rebelled. They smuggled in forbidden books, they even organised strikes. The seminary was a hotbed of political agitation. Young Joseph plunged into all this activity with enthusiasm. He borrowed forbidden texts from the library in the town, and became a star of the frequent student debates. (He had to win, though. If he looked like losing an argument, he became angry and revengeful – another dictator characteristic.)

YOUNG REVOLUTIONARY

Joseph joined a secret socialist organisation in the town, and became one of its keenest members. Soon he was conducting secret revolutionary workshops. As the years went by his political work took over from his studies, and the seminary saw less and less of him. In 1899 he was expelled 'for not attending examinations'. According to Stalin it was really for spreading Marxism – the theories of revolutionary writer Karl Marx.

EXPELLED

Young Joseph Djugashvili spent the next few years pursuing his political studies, gradually moving towards the Bolsheviks who were the revolutionary side of the Socialist Party. To support himself, and to cover his revolutionary activities, he took a job as a clerk at the Tiflis Observatory.

In 1901 the Bolsheviks planned to defy the authorities and openly celebrate May Day, the big Socialist festival. The secret police got word of it, and decided to strike first. Joseph's room was raided, and he narrowly escaped capture. He went on the run.

ON THE RUN

For the next ten years he was to live the life of a full-time revolutionary, hiding from the police, using false names and false papers, holding secret meetings, and publishing forbidden underground newspapers and pamphlets. He used a number of names during this time, but the one that stuck was Stalin – the man of steel. Stalin moved on from Tiflis to the nearby town of Batun, spreading socialism and organising strikes amongst the workers.

In 1902 he was arrested and sent to prison. He escaped almost immediately, and was soon back in Tiflis, working for the revolution. He was to be in and out of jail many times in the next few years.

A LITTLE LOVE

There's little to say about Stalin's private life – as a fulltime revolutionary he hardly had time for one. He was married briefly to Ekaterina, the sister of one of his fellow student revolutionaries. Because of his way of life they probably saw little of each other, and she died a few years later.

A LOT OF MONEY

An important part of Stalin's activity was fund-raising. The revolutionaries were desperately short of money and it was decided that the answer was not flag-days but bank raids. Stalin organised 'fighting squads' who relieved the authorities of large amounts of cash. In 1907 for instance, in Tiflis, they liberated a quarter of a million roubles for Bolshevik funds.

RISING STAR

Stalin soon rose to fame amongst the Bolshevik revolutionaries. He became a member of the ruling Central Committee, a protegé of the great Lenin. He was an expert at the political in-fighting so common amongst the Bolsheviks. His greatest rival was Trotsky, for whom he conceived a personal dislike, calling him 'a champion with fake muscles'.

EXILED

Stalin's luck finally ran out in 1913 when he was rounded up and exiled to Siberia for four years. It was a harsh life in a tiny settlement miles from anywhere, unbearably hot in the short summer, freezing cold in the long winter. Not every exile survived Siberia. In 1916 he was summoned for military service, but got off because of his stiff arm.

REVOLUTION

The Communist Revolution of 1917 put an end to his exile.

Stalin made his way to St Petersburg and plunged back into political activity. His rise was rapid. After the October Revolution he became Commissar of Nationalities. In the bitter civil war that followed the Revolution, he defended the town of Tsarvitch so successfully that it was re-named Stalingrad in his honour.

MARRIED TO NADIA

In 1918 Stalin was married again, this time to Nadia, the daughter of a workman who had befriended and helped him.

In 1924 he succeeded Lenin, the architect of the Russian Revolution, as Chairman of the Politburo, highest office of the new Communist state. It's been said that Lenin believed in democracy, although he was forced to use fascist methods to establish it. He disapproved of Stalin who used fascist methods to establish a dictatorship. Political rivals were exiled or killed. (Sometimes both. Trotsky fled to Mexico but it didn't save him from Stalin's messenger – an assassin with an ice-pick.)

DICTATOR

By 1928 Stalin was a virtual dictator. He started his first five year plan for industry, and for the collectivisation of agriculture. The plans were carried out with ruthless efficiency. When they went wrong, millions of Russians died of starvation.

Not that anyone complained. Stalin, like many dictators, was becoming totally paranoid. The slightest sign of opposition resulted in an arrest, a charge of treason, a show trial complete with confession, followed by prison or a death sentence.

NADIA'S TRAGEDY

Stalin's ruthlessness brought tragedy into his private life. Even his devoted wife Nadia came to doubt his policies. She felt guilty because millions of fellow Russians were suffering and dying while she lived a luxurious life in the Kremlin. One evening in 1932, when they were dining at the house of some friends, she spoke out against the famine raging in the country, the harm caused to the Party by her husband's ruthless purges of men who had once been his comrades. The enraged Stalin burst out into a stream of angry abuse. Nadia rushed out of the house, went home, and committed suicide.

This terrible event seems to have shaken even Stalin. Next day at a top level meeting he offered to resign. Whether he actually meant it is impossible to say. What is certain is that no one dared take him up on it. (Many years later, Stalin's daughter, Svetlana, left Russia for the West. She wrote a book called 'Letters to a Friend' giving fascinating details of family life in the Kremlin.)

PURGES AND WAR

Stalin was all too aware of the discontent all around him. His main fear was that the Red Army would turn against him. He decided to strike first. His 1938 purge cost the Army ten thousand senior officers.

He was also aware of the growing menace of Nazi Germany, but his attempts to set up some kind of defence alliance with the West all got the cold shoulder. With cynical realism, Stalin made an alliance with Hitler himself. The Russo-German pact of 1939 was basically an agreement to carve up Poland between them.

Stalin had no illusions that this made Hitler his friend. But even he was surprised when Hitler suddenly attacked Russia in 1941. Stalin became Prime Minister, and Supreme Commander of the Soviet Armed Forces.

UNDER ATTACK

The initial success of the German invasion weakened Stalin's authority, just as his purge had weakened the Red Army. (It's said that Stalin killed off more Russian officers than Hitler ever did.) But as Russian troops held the German armies outside Moscow and defeated them at Stalingrad, Stalin successfully renewed his grip on power.

STALIN'S ALLIES

Now officially a member of the Allies, he tried to persuade them to launch an attack on occupied Europe in 1942 – a second front to take the pressure off Russia. He even threatened to make another alliance with Hitler. Roosevelt and Churchill refused to listen, and the invasion didn't take place until 1944.

At the various Allied conferences in Teheran in 1943, and Yalta and Potsdam in 1945, Stalin emerged as a major figure amongst the Allied leaders. In a sense he had every right. The Russian people made the biggest sacrifices of anyone in what they called the Great Patriotic War. Millions of Russian lives were sacrificed as the Allies built up their strength for D-Day. Russian troops joined the Allies in the capture of Berlin, Russian guns shelled the bunker as Hitler committed suicide.

COLD WAR

After the war everything changed. No longer needing the friendship of his wartime allies, Stalin emerged in his true colours – a ruthless and ambitious tyrant. Russia took over most of Eastern Europe, as well as East Germany, Poland, Hungary and Czechoslovakia. The Cold War, years of hostility between Russia and the West, was under way.

Stalin lived on till 1953, as suspicious and paranoid as ever, fighting off real and imagined enemies on every side. Today the cult that grew up around him is at an end – they've even changed the name of Stalingrad to Volgograd.

REVOLUTIONARY TO TYRANT

Stalin was the product of an exceptionally harsh time in his country's history. He suffered grinding poverty, long years of danger and oppression, and all the horrors of a bloody revolution. Sadly, his long and bitter struggles seem to have stifled his humanity. He became what he had chosen to call himself – a man of steel, without pity or compassion. Somewhere along the way, his desire to better the lot of his fellow Russians changed to a fierce determination to seize and hold on to personal power at any cost.

UNCLE JOE

While the war was on, Stalin was seen in the West as kindly old Uncle Joe with the bushy moustache, the benign twinkle in the eye, and the love of a glass of vodka. (Military and diplomatic visitors to Moscow during the war tell of the Russian leader's determination to drink them under the table.)

His Russian subjects knew Stalin better. Beneath that kindly exterior was a ruthless tyrant. The Russian people made heroic sacrifices in World War Two, suffering more casualties than any of the Allies. It's a pity they had to live for so long under a dictator as ruthless as the fascists they were fighting or the tyrannical Czars they had overthrown.

MUSSOLINI 1883-1945

BAD BOY BENITO

Benito Mussolini was born in Forli in Northern Italy in 1883. His mother, Rosa, was the local schoolmistress and his father, Allessandro, was the blacksmith. Allessandro was a woman-chaser, a boozer, and a firm believer in beatings with a leather strap (see Hitler and Stalin!).

Benito grew up a bright, but wild and unruly, boy. Stocky and powerful, he was always the first to start a fight. At school he had frightened followers, but no real friends. Benito got away with his bullying for a time – but when he drew a knife on another boy and wounded him, he was expelled.

IN TROUBLE AGAIN

Benito was sent to a second school in nearby Forlimpopoli. He was soon in trouble for bullying and fighting, and even another stabbing. (He only got suspended this time – they were obviously a lot more tolerant at Forlimpopoli.)

More suspensions followed, including several for climbing out at night to visit the local brothels. (Mussolini fancied himself as a ladies' man all his life, and never seemed short of girlfriends and mistresses, all of whom he treated very badly.)

Despite a number of narrow shaves, Benito somehow managed to finish school without being expelled.

THE LADIES FALL AT MY FEET! AND IF THEY DON'T, I SHOOT THEM. THEN THEY FALL AT MY FEET!

TEACHER FROM HELL

In 1902 Benito Mussolini became a substitute teacher in the little town of Gualtieri. He took up politics, joining a socialist group and practising public speaking. He also caused a scandal by his love of wine, and by his passionate affair with the wife of an absent soldier. He carried a knife and a knuckleduster to convince any critics of his behaviour, and he stabbed one of his girlfriends in a quarrel. Parents and schoolkids alike were glad when his teacher's contract came to an end. (His class discipline was very good though. Nothing like a knife and a knuckleduster to cut down on talking in class.)

TEACHER FROM HELL

Out of a job, Mussolini made off to Switzerland, escaping local enemies, angry girlfriends, a mountain of debts, and his upcoming military service.

MUSSOLINI HITS BOTTOM

Mussolini had a hard time in Switzerland. He worked as a builder's labourer and left almost immediately – he was never fond of hard work. He took, and soon left, a number of other lowgrade jobs: butcher's boy, labourer, wine merchant's assistant – he lost that one for drinking too much of his boss's wine. When times got really bad, he wasn't above begging, mugging or theft.

He didn't abandon politics, however. He wrote for a socialist newspaper, and for a time he was secretary to a builder's union. He made inflammatory speeches to expatriate Italian workers, and was arrested several times as an agitator and a vagrant.

BACK TO ITALY

By the time he was twenty-one, Mussolini had had enough of Switzerland. Taking advantage of an amnesty he went back to Italy and did his national service.

When he left the Army, Mussolini took other teaching posts, but was soon in trouble for a combination of thuggish behaviour and revolutionary socialism. (Mussolini was never really a credit to the teaching profession. At one school parents kept their kids at home to keep them away from him.)

MUSSOLINI GETS MARRIED

By now his father, Allessandro, was running a pub in Forli, and Mussolini helped out there between jobs. He even found time to get married to a girl called Rachele, the daughter of one of his father's mistresses. This caused another scandal, since there was a distinct possibility he was marrying his own half-sister.

Needless to say, Mussolini didn't let marriage cramp his style. He continued to chase every attractive female in sight.

PRISON AND THE PRESS

Mussolini continued his career as agitator and journalist. In 1911 he got five months in prison for leading a violent protest against the Italian invasion of Libya.

The prison sentence boosted his reputation as a revolutionary and in 1912 Mussolini got his first big break. His socialist colleagues made him editor of the party newspaper. It was called 'Avanti' ('Forwards!').

It was a feeble sort of publication with a small circulation. Mussolini hardened the paper's party line, wrote stirring editorials, and managed to double the circulation. Suddenly he was a success.

BENITO BREAKS AWAY

When Italy entered the First World War on the side of the Allies, the Socialist Party was firmly against it. Mussolini, however, decided that Italy's entry into the war was a good thing. It might even bring about the revolution: 'Only blood makes the wheels of history turn.'

Unable to convince his colleagues, Mussolini resigned from the paper and started one of his own called 'Il Popolo d'Italia' – 'The People of Italy.'

By now Mussolini was beginning to swing from left to right. Although it was supposed to be a socialist paper, 'Il Popolo' was actually subsidised by the government, and by rich industrialists who wanted to make money from Italy entering the war – the very people Mussolini had once called the enemy.

MUSSOLINI GOES TO WAR

In 1915 Mussolini was called up for war service, fighting in the front line against the Austrians. He was an undistinguished soldier, though he later made up many stories about his own heroism. In promotion terms he went one better than Adolf, reaching the rank of sergeant, but he didn't win any medals.

A CRAZY MIXED-UP PARTY

After the war, Mussolini continued his swing to the far right. In 1919 he launched his own version of the fascist movement, a name which had formerly covered many different little groups. Mussolini's fascists were a motley collection of discontented anarchists, communists, catholics, republicans, socialists and even liberals. No-one really knew what the new party's policies were. Mussolini didn't know either – and he didn't care.

POST WAR BLUES

Even though she'd ended up on the winning side, Italy, like Germany, was in a bad way after the First World War. There was a good deal of public disorder and a fear that Italy might be ripe for a Russian-style communist revolution.

Mussolini formed an army of thugs, the Blackshirts, to preserve public order – in other words, to promote his political policies and beat up his enemies.

QUICK MARCH

In 1922 Mussolini prepared to strike. Assembling his Blackshirts he demanded that the fascists be included in the government 'to restore law and order.' The revolt was a feeble affair that could easily have been crushed by the Army – if the king gave the order. But the king, Victor Emmanuel III was a timid soul. He was afraid of socialists and communists, and didn't trust liberals. He decided to agree to Mussolini's demands. There followed Mussolini's famous 'March on Rome', as the fascists called it. This consisted of a short train-ride for Mussolini (his Blackshirts did all the marching) followed by a victory parade.

FASCIST TAKEOVER

With the king's consent, Mussolini formed a right-wing coalition government, giving himself the title of 'Il Duce' ('The Leader'), and introducing the 'please may I be excused?' fascist salute. (Two ideas later pinched by the admiring Adolf.)

He set up a one-party state, with power concentrated in the Duce and his fascist Grand Council. All opposition was ruthlessly suppressed. Socialism, communism, and even democracy were forbidden. What mattered was unquestioning obedience to the will of Il Duce.

RIVAL RULERS

Hitler finally came to power in 1933. At first Mussolini was jealous of his German disciple, but in a series of meetings Hitler's hypnotic charm won him round. The results were to be a disaster for Italy, as Mussolini was dragged along in the wake of Adolf's mad schemes.

UNEASY ALLIES

When the Second World War started, Mussolini joined in on his fellow dictator's side, although he hung about for a while to make sure Hitler was going to win. When France collapsed, Mussolini thought he was on to a sure thing. Italian troops invaded the south of France. (They found the Germans had pinched all the best spots on the beach.)

Mussolini's later efforts didn't work out any better. His heroic Italian troops invaded Greece by way of Albania, and immediately began doing what they did best – running away. The indignant Greeks chased them right out of Greece, and out of most of Albania as well. Hitler had to send German troops to bail out his Italian ally.

Then the British invaded Abyssyinia, now Ethiopia, and the Italians, who were in practice by now, ran away yet again. Once again Hitler had to come to the rescue. He was finding his Italian friend a bit of a liability.

WHAT A LOUSY WAR

Mussolini then declared war on America – that must have really terrified Roosevelt. After that things went from bad to worse for the unlucky Italians. By 1942 Italy's merchant fleet had been pretty well wiped out and there were terrible food shortages. Mussolini rashly sent Italian troops to help Hitler at the Russian front. Soon they were freezing to death with their defeated German allies, cursing the absence of vino and pasta.

In Italy itself, anti-fascist feeling was growing. There were strikes in lots of the big cities.

In 1943 the Allied powers invaded Sicily, with the enthusiastic help of the Mafia, who'd been given a hard time by Mussolini for years. He'd almost stamped out the Mafia by sending fascist troops to Sicily with orders to lock up anyone who looked villainous and unshaven – which meant most of the male population. (Bashing the Mafia and making the trains run on time were the only real achievements of Mussolini's fascist regime.)

CHANGING SIDES

It was clear to most Italians by now that defeat was only a matter of time. Very few of them had been really keen on the war in the first place. (It interfered with the things Italians are good at – important things, like having lunch, designing cars and clothes, and pinching pretty women.) After a meeting of the Fascist Grand Council Mussolini was deposed as dictator and arrested. The King appointed Marshal Badoglio Prime Minister, and the Marshal declared war on Germany. With typical flair, Italy had changed sides in the middle of a war.

OTTO DROPS IN

Mussolini was held prisoner in a hotel in the Abruzzi mountains. In one of the war's most amazing events, Otto Skorzeny, Germany's top commando, dropped in with a crack parachute squad and pulled off a daring rescue. (Considering how much trouble Mussolini had been, it's a wonder Adolf didn't let the Allies keep him.)

AN UNHAPPY END

Mussolini's rescue proved to be no more than a postponement. He ruled a pocket republic in a German-controlled bit of Italy for two more years. As Germany collapsed, Allied troops came ever closer.

By 1945 even Mussolini realised the game was up. He attempted to flee to Switzerland taking only basic necessities with him – like his long-time mistress, Clara Petacci. They were captured by anti-fascist partisans on the shores of Lake Como. Next day they were shot. Their dead bodies were put on public display in Milan, hanging upside-down from lamp-posts. People came for miles just to spit on them.

TIN-POT TYRANT

A bully-boy from the first, all Mussolini really wanted was power. He loved wearing flashy uniforms and making speeches to cheering crowds. In time he began believing his own lies and lost touch with reality. He invented a new calendar, with the year of his fascist takeover as Year One. Nobody used it. He thought his air-force was twice as big as it was. When he'd inspected one airfield, the planes took off and flew to another, so Mussolini could drive up and inspect them again. He even set up a cardboard cut-out of himself behind the lighted windows of his palace, so the Italian people would think he never slept. He declared war on Italian flies – and the flies won.

Even though Mussolini started his career as the biggest, baddest fascist dictator of all, he ended up as little more than a bad joke. He was a war-loving dictator – and a totally incompetent military leader who lost every battle he ever fought. Through sheer vanity, and a dumb determination to keep up with the Germans, he dragged his country into a war that cost millions of Italian lives. Small wonder his own easy-going countrymen finally turned on him and destroyed him.

SHOOTING STARS

We've covered the leading actors in the drama of World War Two. Now it's time to turn our attention to the other players. And we're not talking about walk-ons. These people were superstars in their own right. Quite a few of them could be called prima-donnas as well — colourful characters with outstanding egos of their own.

Surprisingly, however, one of the most important was one of the least flamboyant — a quiet, shy, genuinely modest man, who rose to the highest positions in both war and peace. A man called Ike...

EISENHOWER 1890-1969

It shows what a mixture of nations make up America – one of the most famous of American generals had a German name...

A BOY CALLED IKE

Despite his name, Dwight David Eisenhower was very much the all-American boy. He was born in Denison, Texas, in 1890, and raised in Abilene, Kansas – a small-town boy and a real mid-Westerner. His parents were humble and hard-up. His father David worked in a creamery, his mother Ida ran the small family farm.

Third of their six sons, young Dwight grew up to be a tall, gangling, easy-going lad, keen on sports and all kinds of outdoor activities. At school he was hard-working, but by no means brilliant. Since his first name was a bit of a mouthful, he soon got a nickname instead. Everyone called him Ike. If there was anything unusual about the boy, it was the way he always seemed to get on well with people. Everyone liked Ike.

WEST POINT IKE

Ike applied for a place at West Point, the American equivalent to Sandhurst, entering in 1911. It wasn't that he was all that keen on the Army, but the family was hard-up. West Point offered a free college education and a chance to play football.

Raised in a big family, and well-used to hard work, Ike enjoyed West Point. He made friends, and played a lot of football, coaching fellow-students as well as being on the team. A bit too easy-going for his instructors' taste, Ike was frequently in trouble for such minor sins as unauthorised smoking and an untidy room. He graduated in 1915, 61st in a class of 164. A long way from top, but comfortably up in the top half. Good old average Ike...

IKE'S EARLY DAYS

Commissioned as a second lieutenant in the infantry, Ike became a supply officer at Fort Sam Houston in Texas. In 1916 he married a nice all-American girl called Mary, the daughter of a wealthy businessman. She had a nickname too – everyone called her Mamie.

The young couple settled down to married life on an army post. Even America's entry into the war in 1917 didn't disturb things too much. Ike was posted to Fort Oglethorpe, Georgia, where he helped to train officer candidates. Later he transferred to the Tank Corps, where they gave him another training job. Although he gained a lot of valuable administrative experience, Ike went through World War One without hearing a single shot fired – something his rivals brought up against him later.

THE LONG SLOG

After the war career prospects weren't exactly brilliant for a very average young officer with no combat experience. Ike didn't complain. Cheerful and hard-working as ever, he got on with the jobs he was given. He got his routine promotions, to lieutenant and to captain. By 1920 Ike had reached the rank of major – where he stuck for the next twenty years. In a peace-time army, promotion can be very, very slow...

IKE'S BIG BREAK

In 1925 Ike had something of a break. He was selected for a place at the Staff College, a sort of army university for ambitious officers. Ike had learned a lot during ten years of soldiering. In 1926 he graduated first, in a class of 275.

His reward was another administrative job, worthy but unexciting. He became assistant to General Pershing, head of the Monuments Commission. Ironically he was given the job of compiling a guide to American battlefields of World War One – the battlefields on which Ike had never fought. Conscientious as ever, Ike did a good job. General Pershing was impressed.

THE WAY UP

Ike continued his steady and unspectacular climb, moving through a variety of administrative posts. He became an executive assistant to the Assistant Secretary for War, making plans to turn peacetime industry over to war work. He worked for the flamboyant General Douglas MacArthur, the Chief of Staff.

By now it was the forties. There was war in Europe, and the American Army was expanding fast. Ike became Chief of Staff, first for the Third Division, then for the Ninth Army Corps. The long delayed promotions came quickly now. He became a full colonel in March 1941. By September he was a brigadier-general.

IKE TAKES OVER

By the time America entered the war, Ike had built up an

invaluable reputation as a first-class administrator and a hardworking staff officer who got the job done without fuss or complaint. General Marshal chose him for Assistant Chief of Staff, and head of the War Plans Division.

By 1942 the American government was getting worried about poor relations between the Americans and their English allies. Ike was promoted to Major-General and put in command of the US Army in Europe. The unassuming administrator was at the very centre of the war.

DIPLOMAT IKE

Ike was the perfect man for the job. The British, who up till now had born the brunt of the war, were inclined to be suspicious and somewhat resentful of the newly-arriving Americans. (The ordinary British soldier grumbled that the newcomers were 'over-paid, over-sexed and over here!')

Working 18 hours a day, Ike started sorting things out and smoothing things over. He ordered newly arriving American troops to be briefed on how to get on with their British hosts. He didn't only have difficult and excitable allies, like Britain's Churchill and France's de Gaulle to deal with. He had almost as much trouble from ambitious American generals like Patton. Sometimes he must have felt the Germans were the least of his worries. Ike's charm and his gift for compromise and conciliation usually won the day. The so-called Allies were always arguing – but they all liked Ike.

WE ALL LIKE IKE!

THREE CHEERS FOR IKE!

IKE OVERSEAS

In 1942 Ike was chosen to lead the Allied attack on North Africa – 'Operation Torch'. It was the first really big combined operation. Inexperienced in combat as he was, Ike had to coordinate the whole thing, juggling the efforts of British, American and French operations on land, sea and air. It was all a tremendous strain and Ike found consolation in the company of his driver, an attractive Anglo-Irishwoman called Kay Summersby. They became very good friends – quite how good no-one was sure. They were certainly very close, and Ike kept her at his side, wherever he went, for most of the war. (Long after the war Kay Summersby published a book called 'Past Forgetting' claiming they'd had a long-lasting love affair.)

In less than a year the conquest of Tunisia was completed. In 1943, Ike, now a full general, commanded the Allied forces in the successful invasion of Sicily, followed by that of Italy itself.

IKE AND OVERLORD

In December 1943 Ike was given the biggest job of all – to command Supreme Headquarters, Allied Expeditionary Force (SHAEF, for short) and plan the Allied invasion of Occupied Europe. It was an almost impossibly complex task, the build-up, training and preparation of an immense multi-national force.

Once again Ike oversaw the whole thing, keeping the peace amongst all the different commanders and interfering politicians. On June 6th 1944, with the invasion already delayed, sea-sick troops waiting on transport ships in the channel and the weather looking distinctly dodgy, Ike, all alone, made the most important single decision of the war – to go ahead with the invasion.

ON TO VICTORY

Once the invasion force had fought its way off the beaches, Eisenhower restrained the impatient General Patton, and the even more impatient General Montgomery, both of whom wanted to dash ahead with their respective armies. He ordered a steady broadfront advance.

EISENHOWER RESTRAINED THE IMPATIENT
PATTON AND MONTGOMERY...

Ike remained in command as the Allied armies crossed the Rhine into Germany and drove forwards to Berlin.

After the German surrender in 1945, Ike commanded the American Occupation Zone in Germany. He became Chief of Staff in 1945, retired from the Army in 1948, and was recalled to become Supreme Allied Commander, Europe in 1950.

PRESIDENT IKE

It had been an amazing career and it wasn't over yet.

In 1952 Ike resigned his commission at last and became the Republican candidate for the presidency of the United States. His campaign slogan read simply 'I like Ike!'

The American electorate liked Ike too. He won the 1952 election by a comfortable margin, and won a second term in 1956.

After his second term as President, Dwight Eisenhower retired from public life in 1961. He died in 1969 after a long illness.

GOOD OLD IKE

Ike was a quiet, genuinely modest man, devoted to his duty, a brilliant organiser and a talented diplomat. It's difficult to think of anyone else who could have held the ever-squabbling Allies together and led them to their final victory.

In a world where it's so often the ruthless, pushy egotists who rise to the top, Eisenhower's astonishing success makes a pleasant change. But then, everyone liked Ike...

MONTGOMERY 1887–1976

THE AMAZING MONTY

You couldn't ask for a bigger contrast than between the laidback Ike and the energetic Monty. If there's one word for Montgomery, it's keen! Small and wiry, he was a fox-terrier of a man, bursting with energy, wearing out his friends even more than his enemies. 'In defeat unbeatable – in victory, unbearable!' said Winston Churchill.

MONTY... A FOX-TERRIER OF A MAN

Bernard Law Montgomery was fourth of the nine children of the Bishop of Tasmania, where he spent much of his childhood. 'I was the bad boy of the family, the rebellious one,' wrote Monty later. Young Monty clashed not with his dad the bishop, but with his far more formidable mum. 'She made me afraid of her when I was a child...There was an absence of affectionate understanding.'

Monty remained a rebel all his life.

THE BISHOP OF TASMANIA WITH HIS SON, MONTY
(A TASMANIAN DEVIL ?)

SCHOOL AND SANDHURST

The family came back to England in 1901 and young Bernard was sent to St Paul's School. At school Monty was good at games, especially cricket and rugby, but not much of a scholar. By making a special effort, he managed to get into Sandhurst in 1907.

Sandhurst suited Monty and he was soon promoted to lance corporal cadet. In a stupid practical joke, he set fire to the shirt-tails of a fellow cadet. The cadet was badly burned and Monty was almost expelled. It was Mum who saved the day. She went to see the Commandant of Sandhurst and persuaded him to change his mind. Monty got off with being stripped of his stripe. He finally passed out of Sandhurst in 1908, and joined the Ist Battalion, The Royal Warwickshire Regiment, stationed in Peshawar.

NORTH-WEST FRONTIER

Here, on the famous North-West Frontier, Monty rode and hunted and learned to be a soldier. A nineteenth century soldier, that is – he said later that he never learned anything that would be of the slightest use in a modern war. And war was coming. In 1914 Monty, now a lieutenant, arrived with his regiment in France.

MONTY'S WAR (I)

Three days after his arrival in France Lieutenant Montgomery was at the front, fighting in the battle of Mons.

World War One made a deep impression on Monty – an impression of muddle and mess. Communications were terrible, command was confused. Monty led an attack on a machine-gun nest, armed with a sword. Actually, the sword saved his life. He tripped over it and the enemy bullets went over his head. Most of his men were mown down and the rest ran away.

Monty led a rather more successful infantry charge a little later – successful until Monty was wounded in the lung, and sent home to England by hospital train. He was later awarded the Distinguished Service Cross. Monty made a good recovery, and was back at the front a year later, serving as a staff-officer.

LESSONS OF WAR

During this time, Monty became convinced of the need for clear orders, efficient communications, and well-defined objectives. Above all you had to look after your men. He had no time for heroics, and despised what he called 'stunt merchants.'

'The whole art of war,' wrote Monty, 'is to gain your objective with as little loss as possible.' He decided that when he was in charge – and he was determined to be in charge one day – things would be run very differently.

MONTY'S PEACE

After the war, Monty got himself sent to the staff college at Camberley, and immediately made himself unpopular arguing with the instructors. He got sent to Ireland to serve during the early Troubles, and was then shunted off to a backwater job in a territorial regiment. But Monty wouldn't give in, bombarding his superiors with letters, essays and pamphlets on the art of war. Eventually the Army sent him back to Camberley as an instructor, with the rank of lieutenant colonel.

MONTY GETS MARRIED

Monty decided it was time to get married and looked round for a suitable candidate. He fixed on a beautiful seventeen-year-old girl called Betty Anderson, who he met on holiday in France, and started a determined courtship. Monty had an odd way of wooing. He took the poor girl for long walks on the beach and drew military maps in the sand.

Strangely enough, the beautiful Betty didn't fancy marrying an odd-looking, bossy little man, twenty years older than she was, who never talked about anything but war. Undeterred, Monty joined her on a skiing holiday and proposed. She turned him down.

MONTY WOOS BETTY NO. 1

Fortunately there was a more suitable candidate close at hand. On that very same skiing holiday Monty met another Betty, Betty Carver, an army widow of his own age with two young sons.

They had a great deal in common, they struck up a friendship, and before long they were married.

HAPPINESS AND TRAGEDY

The second Betty was a mature, intelligent woman with an interest in the Arts – which were pretty much a closed book to Monty. She did a great deal to humanise him and broadened his mental horizons. They were happily married for ten years, and had a son called David. 'It had never before seemed possible that such love and affection could exist,' wrote Monty later.

One summer Betty was bitten by a mosquito on a holiday beach. From this trivial infection, blood poisoning set in. Betty became seriously ill and suddenly died. Monty was heartbroken. When he recovered he plunged back into work more obsessively than ever.

He served in India as an instructor at the Quetta Staff College, and in Palestine, suppressing an Arab revolt with ruthless efficiency. Back in Britain in 1939, he was made Commanding General of the Third Division – just in time. A few days later Britain was at war.

MONTY'S WAR (II)

Monty took his men to France with the British Expeditionary Force – and brought them back again after Britain's defeat and evacuation at Dunkirk. Monty didn't think Dunkirk was a heroic feat. He thought it was a disaster. He thought the whole invasion had been a total cock-up, and he stormed into the War Office and said so. The BEF, he said, had never been properly led since it was formed.

He told Churchill so too, over lunch. New and younger commanders were needed – such as himself. 'I don't drink, I don't smoke and I'm a hundred per cent fit!' boasted Monty.

Winston puffed at his cigar, and took a swig of brandy. 'I smoke, I drink and I'm two hundred per cent fit!'

Churchill didn't take to Monty much, calling him, 'A little man on the make' – but he took note of his advice.

TRAINING FOR BATTLE

In 1940 Monty was promoted to Corps Commander. Immediately he started to shake things up. The Army found itself in tough training for the expected German attack – even desk-bound staff officers had to turn out for five mile runs. Inefficient officers were ruthlessly sacked. 'Completely and utterly useless,' snapped Monty – and off they went.

Moving from one command to another, Monty trained Britain's troops for the next two years. But he was still denied what he wanted most of all – to command his men in battle. For all his undoubted efficiency, Monty was almost totally lacking in tact. He'd got up the collective nose of nearly all his superior officers, and unpopularity held him back.

OFF TO AFRICA

It took an unexpected death to give Monty his chance. By now British troops were fighting in Africa – and not doing too well against Rommel, the now-legendary German general. Churchill decided the Eighth Army needed a new commander, and appointed General Gort. But Gort was killed when his plane was shot down, and a reluctant Winston was persuaded to send Monty.

CHURCHILL AND MONTY

When Monty arrived in Africa, morale was low. Rommel was building up his forces for a big new attack. Not many people believed the Eighth Army could stop him and plans were being made for retreat. Monty was appalled by all this defeatism. He summoned his headquarters staff, and announced that all plans to retreat were cancelled. 'We will stand and fight here. If we can't stay here alive, then let us stay here dead.'

HITTING ROMMEL FOR SIX

Monty announced that they were going to 'Hit Rommel and his army for six, right out of Africa... We are going to finish with this chap Rommel once and for all. It will be quite easy. There is no doubt about it. He is definitely a nuisance. Therefore, we will hit him a crack and be rid of him.'

Churchill visited the Eighth Army only six days later, and was amazed by the improvement in spirit. But privately Churchill had his doubts. Could Monty really deliver a victory?

He could and he did. Monty dug in, protecting his few remaining tanks with minefields, anti-tank guns, infantry and massive air cover. When Rommel's Panzers attacked, the Eighth Army hurled them back. Two months later, Monty counter-attacked, decisively defeating Rommel at the Second Battle of El Alamein.

THE FOX-TERRIER CHASES THE DESERT FOX

TOUGH AT THE TOP

It had been some time since the Allies had had a victory and Monty was the hero of the hour. The snappish, sharp-featured little man with two badges in his beret – Monty had added the tank corps badge to his general's badge – suddenly became famous all over the world. But Monty's greatest success marked the beginning of his biggest problems.

War at the top means more than simply good soldiering. It gets mixed up with politics and diplomacy as well. From now on Monty would have to work with the Americans. He had to serve under Eisenhower, a first class administrator and diplomat with almost no experience of battle.

'Nice chap, no general,' said Monty dismissively.

Unrivalled when he was in charge, Monty was all wrong for Anglo-American combined operations. For the rest of the war, he spent almost as much time arguing with the Americans as fighting the Germans. As the Allied armies invaded first Sicily then Italy, Monty gave poor old Ike no end of trouble, arguing over every order he was given. Monty always knew a better way.

What Monty called plain speaking came across to others as rudeness and arrogance. Ike was endlessly patient, but Monty managed to upset most of the other American generals, particularly General Patton, who was as arrogant and ambitious as Monty himself.

D-DAY

Monty's greatest challenge was still to come. When Eisenhower was appointed Supreme Commander of Overlord, the Allied invasion of Nazi-occupied Europe, Monty became his field deputy, commander of all ground forces. For all Monty's outspokenness, Ike recognised that he was still the best man for the job.

Back in England Monty set about training and inspiring the three million British, American and Canadian troops under his command. On June 6th 1944 the armies set sail, supported by six hundred ships and ten thousand planes. After a savage struggle on the Normandy beaches the Allied armies fought their way inland.

TROUBLE AHEAD

There was hard fighting ahead – and fierce quarrelling between Monty and his allies, especially after Eisenhower took over as commander of ground forces in August 1944. Monty wanted to thrust forwards to Berlin, Eisenhower ordered a steady broad front advance. Monty backed the Arnhem operation, an ambitious plan to capture bridges behind enemy lines in Holland by using paratroops. The relief troops failed to arrive in time and Monty accused Eisenhower of not supporting him properly.

MONTY GOES TOO FAR

Suddenly the retreating Germans swung round and staged a massive counter-attack, throwing back the astonished Allies in the Battle of the Bulge. Everyone panicked – everyone but Monty.

Taking charge, he mounted a superb defence in the Ardennes. Once again, Monty was the hero of the hour. Then, typically, he had to go and spoil things. Over-inflated by his undoubted success, he ticked off America's General Bradley, accusing him of inefficiency. Tactless as ever, Monty claimed to have 'saved the Americans', and demanded sole command of the Allied attack on Germany.

Eisenhower had had enough. He threatened to cable Washington, saying either Monty went or he did. The Americans were contributing three-quarters of the men and supplies to the invasion by now, and they weren't going to have some stroppy little Brit telling them what to do. Faced with disgrace and replacement, Monty had the sense to climb down. He made Ike a handsome apology, and promised to behave better in future.

GERMANY SURRENDERS

The Allied advance went on. Monty was still convinced that Eisenhower was handling things all wrong, by being far too slow to move in on Berlin. However, Monty had his moment of triumph. On May 4th 1945, Admiral Doenitz, Hitler's successor, sent representatives to Monty's headquarters on Luneberg Heath, to sue for peace. Monty lined them up on parade, made them salute the Union Jack, and insisted on the total surrender of all enemy forces in northern Germany, Holland and Denmark.

AFTER THE WAR

Monty was showered with honours after the war. Already a Field-Marshal, he was created Viscount Montgomery of Alamein. He served as Chief of the Imperial Staff, and as Deputy Supreme Allied Commander Europe until 1958 when he retired.

Retirement didn't make Monty any less troublesome. Never the over-modest sort, old age made him vainer than ever. In 1958 he published his war memoirs, revealing how little he thought of Eisenhower as a commander, attacking other English and American generals, and pointing out how he'd always been right and everyone else wrong. There was an immediate uproar.

After that Monty travelled the world, writing books and articles, interviewing foreign leaders and telling them where they were going wrong in running their countries.

END OF AN OLD SOLDIER

Monty's final years were lonely, as his health declined. In 1978, just before he died he told a visiting friend that he was worried about the after-life. 'I shall have to meet all those soldiers I got killed, at Alamein and in Normandy.'

Monty's achievements were much argued about after the war. Some military historians say he was simply our best general ever. Others call him over-cautious and over-rated.

A German field-marshal said, 'Generals are like race-horses. They're expected to win – and Monty mostly won.'

There's no doubt that Monty could be arrogant, overbearing, and something of a bully. But he was a good soldier, the supreme professional. Monty saw war as a nasty but necessary job, to be carried out efficiently and with minimum loss of life.

It's a pretty good attitude for a general – ask any soldier.

ROMMEL 1891-1944

An odd thing about the British character is the way we admire our enemies – well, some of them, anyway. Maybe it's something to do with our well-known sporting spirit.

Erwin Rommel, popularly known as 'The Desert Fox', seems to be everyone's favourite German general. (He was even played by James Mason, in the movie of the same name.)

How did this come about? It's a strange story – with an unexpected and terrible end.

ERWIN'S EARLY DAYS

Erwin Rommel was born on November 19th, 1891, in Heidenheim, a small town in Wurttemburg. He was the son of a schoolmaster. There were five children in the family, two older sisters and two younger brothers, with Erwin in the middle.

Little Erwin was a cheerful and friendly child, although at first rather small and pale. At school he was quiet and dreamy, taking no great interest in his studies. In his teens he was very keen on cycling and skiing. Although he never became very tall, he grew up sturdy and tough, with exceptional stamina.

He was very interested in aircraft and built lots of model aeroplanes. With the help of some friends he even built a fullsize glider but it never got off the ground.

ROMMEL'S CAREER GETS OFF TO A NON-FLYING
START WHEN HIS HOME-MADE GLIDER FAILS TO
GET OFF THE GROUND.

ERWIN JOINS UP

Rommel's early ambition was to be an engineer and he planned
to follow a friend working in the Zeppelin factory. (Zeppelins
were a form of early airship.) When his father refused
permission, young Rommel joined the Army instead.

In a way it was a strange decision. In those days the German
Army was dominated by the aristocratic Prussian officer class,
and Rommel's father and grandfather were modest middle-class
teachers. Without influence from family or friends, young
Rommel would have to make it on merit. In 1910 he joined an
infantry regiment as an officer cadet. After a year's compulsory
service in the ranks he was posted to officer school in Danzig
in 1911.

ROMMEL IN LOVE

In Danzig, Rommel met the love of his life. Lucie Maria Mollin was at college there, studying languages. Introduced by a friend, they fell in love. Despite this distraction, Rommel worked hard at his officer school, and passed his exams with good marks.

In 1912 he was commissioned as a second lieutenant, and posted back to his regiment. He wrote to Lucie every day.

Rommel settled down to work as a young second lieutenant. His fellow officers found him a nice enough chap, but a bit of a sobersides. Rommel didn't drink or smoke, and he was almost obsessively keen on his job – not unlike a young officer called Montgomery, over in England. Unlike the flamboyant and opinionated Monty however, Rommel was the quiet type, preferring to get on with the job without fuss – just a good, reliable young officer.

ROMMEL'S WAR (I)

It was the outbreak of World War One that gave Rommel a chance to shine. He turned out to be a born soldier, daring, ruthless and determined. On his first patrol with only a few men, he ran into a much larger force of the enemy. Outnumbered as he was, Rommel attacked at once, taking the enemy by surprise and driving them into cover. He earned the Iron Cross for capturing a blockhouse behind the enemy lines.

Several times wounded, Rommel was promoted to lieutenant and transferred to a mountain battalion. In 1916 he went back to Danzig on leave and married his Lucie. They were to be happily married for the rest of his life.

Rommel spent most of the war fighting in Romania and Italy, steadily adding to his reputation. The climax to his career came at the battle of Caporetto. After days of heavy fighting, Rommel and a few of his men scaled a sheer mountain face to reach the HQ of the Salerno brigade, and bluffed the astonished Italians into surrendering. In just a few days, Rommel had captured 9000 men and over 80 guns. He was decorated again and promoted to captain. He served on the staff until Germany's defeat in 1918.

BETWEEN WARS

Rommel had returned a hero. But with Germany's defeated Army deliberately kept small by the victorious Allies, his career prospects looked slim. He commanded an internal security company for a while, encountering some revolutionary soldiers who booed him for wearing his medals and wanted to appoint a commissar. Rommel said he proposed to command soldiers, not criminals, and they soon fell into line. After that bit of excitement, Rommel served as a regimental officer for the next ten years.

In 1929 Rommel was posted as an instructor to the infantry school at Dresden. He stayed there for four years, delivering lectures and writing a book on infantry tactics. In 1933 the Nazis came to power with Hitler as Chancellor. Things in Germany – and in the German Army – were about to change.

HITLER'S GENERAL

A dedicated soldier, Rommel was basically non-political. He didn't think much of the Nazis, describing them as 'a set of scallywags'. But Hitler had one aim of which Rommel thoroughly approved – the expansion of the Army. Fiercely patriotic, Rommel believed Germany wouldn't be better treated until she was strong again. So, like most military men, he went along with Hitler.

Under the militaristic Nazi regime, promotions started coming more quickly. Before long Rommel, now a lieutenant colonel, became an instructor at the War Academy at Potsdam. Three years later he was promoted to colonel and appointed to the command of Hitler's special bodyguard. The job brought him to the attention of the Fuehrer. In 1939 Rommel became a brigadier general.

ROMMEL'S WAR (II)

When the Second World War broke out, Rommel was keen to be back in action. He asked Hitler for a field command, and in 1940 he was given command of the Seventh Panzer Division.

ROMMEL'S CAREER REALLY TAKES OFF (SO TO SPEAK)
WHEN HE IS GIVEN COMMAND OF THE SEVENTH PANZER
DIVISION.

Rommel soon proved himself a master of tank warfare. His Panzer division took part in Hitler's Blitzkrieg, the lightning attack through Belgium into France. Rommel's Panzers raced to cut off the retreating British Army at Dunkirk. Hitler ordered them to halt – no-one quite knows why.

In January 1941, Rommel was promoted to major general and given command of the newly formed Afrika Korps, a force formed to help the Italians fight the British in North Africa.

Rommel went on to the attack almost as soon as he arrived in Africa. Taking the British by surprise, he drove them back. The British rallied and pushed Rommel back to Benghazi. Suddenly, Rommel mounted a lightning counter-attack, re-capturing Benghazi and driving the British clear out of the area called Cyrenaica. Then he flew back to Berlin to see Hitler, asking for reinforcements to follow up his advantage. Hitler refused. He was preoccupied with the invasion of Russia – Africa was just a side show. Undeterred, Rommel returned to Africa and attacked Tobruk. He captured it in June 1942, after four weeks of bitter fighting.

THE DESERT FOX

By now Rommel had built up a pretty awesome reputation. The British were getting worried – so much so that General Auchinleck, the Commander-in-Chief, sent a special order out to all his officers. 'There exists a real danger that our friend Rommel is becoming a kind of magician or bogeyman to our troops...He is by no means a superman, although he is undoubtedly very energetic and able. Even if he were a superman, it would still be very undesirable that our men should credit him with supernatural powers...'

Luckily for the British the situation was about to change.

ENTER MONTY

A new general called Montgomery took over, who wasn't in the least bothered about Rommel's reputation. The British built up their defences, and the next time Rommel's forces attacked they were thrown back. Rommel became seriously ill and had to be sent back to Berlin on sick leave. Montgomery attacked in force. Rommel hurriedly returned to the front, but it was too late. Hitler had starved him of men, tanks and supplies, and the British and their American allies had built up an overwhelmingly superior force.

Hitler ordered Rommel to fight to the last man – but Rommel had no intention of wasting his soldiers' lives. Fighting a series of rearguard actions, he retreated to Tunisia. Hitler ordered him to fly back to Berlin. Two months after Rommel's departure, his entire army surrendered.

THE DESERT FOX GOES TO GROUND

ROMMEL FIGHTS ON

Although he was now out of favour with Adolf, Rommel was too good a general to waste. He was sent to Italy to organise the Italians – never an easy task – and then to Greece. In 1944 he was sent to occupied France to help prepare for the Allied invasion. Guessing, quite correctly, that Normandy was the most likely attack-point, Rommel set about strengthening coastal defences.

The D-day invasion duly came on the 6th of June 1944. Rommel knew that his only chance was to keep the Allied armies pinned down on the beaches. He asked Hitler to release the Panzer reserves, but know-it-all Adolf refused. Hitler had fallen for the Allies deception plan. He was convinced the Normandy attack was a bluff and the real invasion would take place at Calais.

Rommel had been right – the Normandy attack was the real invasion. The Allies fought their way off the beaches and moved on inland.

ROMMEL DISILLUSIONED

Being right when Hitler was wrong made Rommel more unpopular with Adolf than ever. But by now Rommel himself had pretty well had enough of Hitler. On his return from Africa he had learned of the atrocities in Russia and eastern Europe, and of the full horror of the Holocaust, Hitler's plan to exterminate the Jews. Shocked, Rommel went to see Hitler to protest. 'If such things go on,' he said, 'we shall lose the war.' Rommel suggested that the Gestapo should be disbanded, and the SS split up and mixed with regular troops. Not surprisingly, Hitler wouldn't listen.

By now Rommel realised that Germany had no hope of winning the war. He also knew that there was no hope of peace while Hitler was in charge. When a group of like-minded generals approached him, Rommel agreed to a number of meetings, to discuss what could be done. The plan was for Rommel to replace Hitler, and negotiate peace with the Allies.

THE GENERAL'S PLOT

Still thinking things over, Rommel went off on a tour of inspection. His staff car was attacked by British fighters, and he was badly wounded.

Three days later, while Rommel was still recovering, Hitler too narrowly escaped death – from a bomb planted in his headquarters by one of the plotters. Badly shaken, but not badly hurt, Hitler began hunting down his attackers. There were thousands of arrests and executions. One of the plotters made a bungled attempt at suicide. Delirious, he mentioned Rommel's name. For Hitler that was evidence enough.

In fact, although Rommel had known of the assassination plot, he had opposed it. Why make a martyr of Hitler, he had argued. The man should be arrested and brought to trial by the Army.

A HERO'S DEATH

Recovering from his wounds at his home in Herrlingen, Rommel received a visit from two Nazi generals, who arrived in a car with an SS driver. They brought a gift from Adolf Hitler – a poison capsule for Rommel.

If Rommel agreed to take poison, the German people would be

told he had died of his wounds. He would have a hero's death and a state funeral – and his wife and son would be unharmed.

If Rommel refused to commit suicide, he would be brought to trial as a traitor, found guilty and executed. Under Nazi law, his family would be considered traitors too. They would be arrested, probably even executed.

For Rommel there was no choice. Putting on his old Afrika Korps uniform, he said goodbye to his wife and son and went off with his sinister visitors in their car. Twenty-five minutes later, there was a phone call from the local hospital. Tragic news: General Rommel had been taken ill while out driving, and had died before he reached hospital.

For what it was worth, Hitler kept his word. Rommel was given a magnificent funeral, with tributes from Adolf and all the top Nazis. His wife and son were unharmed – both survived the war.

OUR FRIEND ROMMEL

Rommel was an honourable man and a superb soldier, adored by both officers and his men. Considerably more modest than his more colourful opponent Monty, Rommel was the supreme professional, with few interests outside his job. He was, said one of his aides, '100 per cent soldier.'

Rommel fought bravely for an evil regime, only turning against it when it was too late. In the glory days in North Africa, before his tragic end, he was respected and even admired by Monty's Desert Rats as an honourable enemy.

THE DESERT RATS ADMIRE THE DESERT FOX

Let Winston Churchill have the last word: 'We have a very skilful opponent against us, and, may I say across the havoc of war, a great general.'

Erwin Rommel would have wanted no better tribute.

GOERING 1893-1946

Not only do we have a favourite German general, we even have a favourite Nazi – though with much less justification.

Hermann Goering was no better than the rest of the Nazi crew. But he did have a little more style...

HEROIC HERMANN

Hard as it is to believe, Hermann Goering began life as a handsome young hero. He was even thin...

He was born in Rosenheim, Upper Bavaria, in 1893, the son of an important colonial official. (Goering was one of the few early Nazis with any claim to being a gentleman.)

Hermann was one of five children, with two brothers and two sisters. Apparently the Goering children were all very well behaved – all except Hermann. He was a sturdy, self-willed little boy, determined to have his own way. When the Boer War was on in South Africa, between the British and the Dutch, Hermann took command of the village boys and formed them into an army, calling himself 'Hermann Goering, General of the Boers.'

HERMANN IN THE ARMY

Hermann remained a rebel throughout his schooldays and his father decided he needed some military discipline. He was sent off to a cadet school at Karlsruhe, then on to a military training college near Berlin. In 1912 he became a second lieutenant in an infantry regiment. He was regarded as an efficient enough young officer, perhaps a bit too full of himself. He had a bad habit of arguing with his superiors.

When war broke out in 1914, Second-Lieutenant Goering was soon in action. His regiment was stationed close to the border, and young Hermann went out on patrol, commanding a force of six men on bicycles. Daring to the point of rashness, he often disobeyed orders, moving behind enemy lines. He made an unsuccessful attempt to kidnap a French general, and ended up capturing four French horses – Hermann always had an eye for loot.

GOERING CAPTURED FOUR FRENCH HORSES

As the war went on, his regiment fought its way into France through the Vosges Mountains. Conditions were harsh and the cold and damp gave Hermann rheumatism in his joints. He was evacuated to hospital in Freiburg in the Black Forest.

HERMANN TAKES OFF

Wondering how to get back to the fighting, Hermann was visited by a friend in the flying corps who suggested a transfer. Hermann took up the idea with enthusiasm. At first the Army refused to agree. Goering made a thorough nuisance of himself. He even forged his own transfer papers, narrowly escaping a court martial. Worn out, the Army finally agreed. In October 1914, Goering joined the Flying Corps.

He flew with the squadron commanded by Von Richtofen, the famous 'Red Baron'. Goering himself became a fighter ace, with twenty-one 'kills' to his credit. When the Red Baron was finally shot down in 1918, Goering, promoted to captain, took command of the squadron.

In 1918 the Kaiser awarded him the 'Orden "Pour le Merite"', Germany's equivalent of the Victoria Cross. By now Hermann was a popular hero. Postcards with his portrait were sold all over Germany, and adoring girls wrote him fan letters.

HERMANN BETWEEN THE WARS

By 1918 Germany had lost the war. Captain Goering came home to a country in chaos. No one had much use for returning heroes. Like many other officers, he was attacked by a revolutionary mob, who tried to tear off his decorations. To make matters worse he was penniless, with no gratuity and no pension.

Cashing in on what remained of his wartime fame, Goering got a job demonstrating German planes at an aeronautical exhibition in Copenhagen. At weekends he made extra money selling joy-rides in country towns. In between flying, he had a high old time in the bars and nightclubs of Copenhagen.

When the money ran out, Goering moved on to Sweden, earning his living as best he could. He sold parachutes, he became a stunt flyer, and a commercial pilot.

HERMANN'S ROMANCE

In 1921 an eccentric Swedish count hired Hermann to fly him back to his castle. They flew through a snowstorm, landing on a lake beside the castle. Made welcome by the Countess, Hermann was introduced to her sister, a dark beauty called Carin. By the time he left the castle, two days later, Goering was in love. Carin felt the same way – despite the fact that she was already married to a captain in the Swedish Army. Over the next few months, they managed further meetings. Goering persuaded Carin to divorce her husband and return to Germany with him.

The Swedish captain took it like a gentleman. There was an amicable divorce, and he even settled some money on his wife to begin her new married life. Hermann had struck lucky.

HERMANN MEETS HITLER

The couple were married in Munich, and Hermann enrolled at the university as a mature student. He started taking an interest in politics. One evening he and his wife went to a meeting of the newly-formed Nazi Party, and heard Hitler speak – and that was it. Goering knew that this was the leader Germany needed. 'I am for that man body and soul,' he told Carin.

Hitler was highly delighted with his new recruit – just what the party needed, a touch of class. 'Splendid! A war hero with the

"Pour le Merite" – imagine it! Excellent propaganda! Moreover, he has money, and doesn't cost me a penny.'

A BAD BEGINNING

At first things went badly for the new Nazi Party. Goering helped to organise Adolf's unsuccessful coup, the Munich Putsch of 1923. He was at Hitler's side when the police opened fire, and the would-be revolutionaries fled. Hitler was arrested and sent to jail. Goering was wounded in the legs and stomach. He was taken to hospital, and later smuggled over the border to Austria.

Goering's wounds were made worse by infection from chips of flying masonry. It took him a long time to recover completely. During the process he became addicted to the morphine doctors gave him to dull the pain.

HERMANN IN EXILE

The Goerings entered on a period of exile, first in Austria and later in Italy. Money was short, and although Goering's health improved, his wife's declined. They went back to Sweden where they were helped by Carin's family. Goering's morphine addiction worsened, and he became unbalanced and often violent. It took several spells in hospital, one of them in the violent ward of a sanatorium, before he was cured.

His health more or less restored, Goering went back into the parachute business. He paid a brief business visit to England, where he offered to lay a wreath on the RAF Memorial. Since he was still technically a political criminal, the embarrassed Air

Ministry put him off, wining and dining him till he forgot all about it.

BACK TO GERMANY

In 1926 the Munich Putsch plotters were given an amnesty. Goering hurried back to re-join Hitler. By now the Nazi Party was recovering from the failed coup and was back on the road to power. Times were hard at first, but Goering worked unceasingly, organising the SA, Hitler's private army, touring the country and making innumerable speeches. His wife Carin, whose health was failing badly by now, said every day was taken up with politics, and most of the night as well.

HERMANN'S CAREER

In 1928 Goering was one of the first Nazis actually elected to the Reichstag, and he was re-elected in 1930. In 1931 Carin died. Goering was genuinely heartbroken, plunging even deeper into politics.

By 1932 Goering was President of the Reichstag. When Hitler became Chancellor in 1933, Goering became Reichsminister for the Air Force, and Prussian Minister of the Interior. He created the Secret State Police, the 'Geheimestaats Poleitzi' – 'Gestapo' for short. He established a concentration camp, the first of many, in Oranienberg, a suburb of Berlin. In 1935 Goering became Commander in Chief of the Air Force.

HERMANN KEEPS CLIMBING

By now Hermann Goering was one of the biggest men in the Nazi Party – in more ways than one. His waistline was swelling with his importance.

He lived in a virtual palace in Berlin, and he had an enormous hunting lodge outside the city. It was called Karinhal, in memory of his first wife. In 1935 he married again. His second wife, Emmy, was a beautiful actress. Since Hitler, despite many offers from adoring females, hung on to his bachelor status, Emmy became top Nazi hostess, First Lady of the Third Reich.

Goering master-minded Hitler's annexation of Austria in 1938, and the later takeover of Czechoslovakia. Something of a moderate in Nazi terms, he didn't want to go to war over Poland, and encouraged negotiations with Neville Chamberlain. Just before war broke out, Hitler named Goering as his official successor.

HERMANN ON TOP

Hermann Goering was now at the top of the Nazi tree, second only to Adolf himself. He was also very rich, and he owned a huge art collection. Goering had also made a fortune, using his political power in dodgy business dealings with state-owned industrial enterprises.

Hermann Goering was at the peak of his fame and popularity, and enjoying every minute of it. He was cheerful and easy-going, unlike his solemn Nazi colleagues, and the people loved him. They delighted in his larger-than-life extravagance, his tantrums and his love of gorgeous uniforms and decorations. The Berliners nick-named him 'Iron Fatty'. As Goering himself said, 'The people need to love and the Fuehrer was often too far from the broad masses. Then they clung to me.'

Hermann was at the high point of his career – then everything started going wrong. It was all the fault of the RAF.

GOERING WAS NOW AT THE TOP OF THE NAZI TREE, SECOND ONLY TO ADOLF HIMSELF.

BATTLE OF BRITAIN BLUES

When the war began in 1939 Goering commanded the Luftwaffe, the German Air Force. In the Blitzkrieg, Hitler's lightning attack on Poland and France, the German pilots did well, partly because of combat experience gained in the Spanish Civil War, which the Nazis had used as a training exercise.

Then came the Battle of Britain – and the beginning of Hermann's downfall. After Britain evacuated what was left of her army at Dunkirk, the next logical step for Germany was an invasion of England. But Hitler's generals refused to consider it without guaranteed superiority in the air. 'Leave it to the Luftwaffe,' said Goering.

They did – and it all went wrong.

THE WURST IS YET TO COME!

'IRON FATTY'

In 1940, Britain's young pilots fought the Luftwaffe to a standstill in the summer skies over England. They were helped by something called radar – a cunning new system for detecting the approach of enemy planes. The struggle in the air became known as the Battle of Britain – and Goering's Luftwaffe lost. The invasion of Britain was postponed – indefinitely.

FROM BAD TO WORSE

Goering reacted to his defeat with windy speeches, promising to crush Britain with a rain of bombs. Then he went on a tour of occupied Europe, adding to his art collection by snaffling masterpieces from all the occupied countries.

As the war went on, Goering's prestige steadily declined – much to the delight of such envious rivals as Himmler, Goebbels and Bormann, all fighting for Hitler's favour.

Goering's duties as leader of the Luftwaffe had been badly neglected. The British and their American allies started to strike back, and Allied bombs rained down on Germany. Low in morale, badly organised, and equipped with largely inferior fighters, the Luftwaffe were powerless to stop them. Goering, who was himself largely responsible for the mess, told his discouraged and defeated pilots that they were a disgrace to Germany. It didn't do much for morale.

THE WAY DOWN

The war continued to go badly for Germany, but by now Goering was taking little real part in it. Ignoring the string of disasters, he lived in a world of his own, travelling in his luxurious private train, adding to his art collection, eating and drinking enormous amounts, and changing in and out of his collection of gorgeous uniforms.

MIRROR MIRROR ON THE FLOOR, WHO IS THE ONE THE GIRLS ADORE?

... CHANGING IN AND OUT OF HIS COLLECTION OF GORGEOUS UNIFORMS.

Disaster did nothing to lessen his enormous conceit. In 1945, when the end was obviously very near, Goering sent a message to Hitler. Maybe it was time for him to take over, suggested Hermann helpfully.

GOERING CAPTURED

It was hardly tactful. Hitler, who was by now beleaguered in his bunker, flew into a screaming rage and ordered Goering to be stripped of all his offices and then shot.

Before the sentence could be carried out, Adolf had committed suicide, and Goering had been captured by the Americans. He immediately demanded a 'man-to-man talk' with Eisenhower. They'd soon sort everything out. To Goering's amazement the demand was refused and he was put on trial with the other Nazi leaders at Nuremburg.

HERMANN ON TRIAL

Flamboyant to the last, Goering more or less took over the trial. Insisting he was senior officer, he demanded that all the other accused obey his orders. He defended himself brilliantly in the dock, saying he knew nothing about the Nazi Party's crimes.

It was hopeless of course. The evidence was overwhelming. Hermann Goering had known of, and supported, every crime committed by the Third Reich, up to and including the Holocaust. 'His guilt is unique in its enormity,' said the judges. 'The record shows no excuses for this man.'

DEATH SENTENCE

Goering was sentenced to death by hanging. Outraged, he demanded a more honourable death – execution by firing squad. This too was refused.

Goering kept his confidence to the very end. In a letter to his wife Emmy he wrote, 'In fifty or sixty years there'll be statues of

Hermann Goering all over Germany,' adding wryly, 'Little statues, maybe...'

Unpredictable to the last, Hermann Goering managed to avoid the hangman. Two hours before he was due to be executed, he was found dead in his cell. Somehow he'd managed to get his hands on a phial of poison. When the news spread, the defeated Germans managed a wry grin. Old Iron Fatty had always enjoyed a joke – even when it was against himself.

GOERING...

GOERING...

GONE.

END OF THE ROAD

Hermann Goering had reached the end of the road that began when he first heard Adolf Hitler speak in a beer hall in Munich. He was a colourful and, in some ways, an oddly likeable man, certainly the only Nazi who showed any sign of a sense of humour. But early heroism and a flamboyant character aren't enough to redeem his leading part in a cruel and evil regime.

GOEBBELS 1897-1945

Joseph Goebbels was a man in advance of his time – history's earliest spin doctor. He was one of the first to realise that mass media can be manipulated to shape political opinion. This sharp-featured, ratty little fellow was a master of propaganda – and a major architect of Adolf Hitler's success.

AN UNLUCKY BEGINNING

Joseph Goebbels was born in the Rhineland town of Rheydt in 1897. His father managed a small textile factory. Joseph's early childhood was happy enough, but when he was still only four he had a stroke of bad luck that ruined much of his later life. He was struck down with polio. It left him with a crippled left foot and a weak left leg. Unable to play with other children, young Joseph grew up to be a bit of a recluse. He became a keen student. If he couldn't be as strong as other kids, at least he could be brighter.

Unfortunately he was embittered by his handicap. As he grew older he developed a sharp tongue, and soon became feared for a constant flow of cutting and critical remarks.

JOSEPH REJECTED

When war broke out in 1914 Joseph, still only seventeen, volunteered for the German Army. Inevitably he was turned down. The rejection increased both his bitterness, and his sense of patriotism. However, the hard work at school paid off. He got a grant that enabled him to study German history, literature and culture, and he attended no less than six universities, ending up at Heidelburg.

JOSEPH JOINS THE PARTY

After university Goebbels struggled to establish himself as a writer and political journalist, supporting himself by a bit of private tuition. In 1922 he heard Hitler speak in Munich, and realised he had found the leader he was looking for. He joined the Nazi Party that same year.

By 1926 Goebbels had risen to be a Gauleiter, or district leader, in Berlin. Success didn't make him any less bitter. Spindly, physically handicapped, suspiciously intellectual, Goebbels didn't fit in too well with the ideal Nazi image of a burly stormtrooper with more brawn than brain. The other Nazi leaders made jokes about him, and called him Doctor Mouse.

...SHARP–FEATURED, RATTY
LITTLE FELLOW...

Nevertheless, the odd-looking little man with the long nose and the ankle-length trenchcoat soon became an important figure in the party. Hitler was so impressed with Goebbels's hard work and organising ability that he appointed him Party Propaganda Leader in 1929.

In 1930 Goebbels made another good career move. He married a beautiful divorcee, a party worker called Magda Quant, who happened to be a particular favourite of Adolf's. The move brought him to the heart of Hitler's circle.

GOEBBELS GETS GOING

Goebbels turned out to have a natural gift for publicity and propaganda. He poured out a stream of leaflets and posters containing vague but impressive slogans:

RESTORATION OF GERMAN HONOUR
DEATH SENTENCE FOR CRIMES AGAINST THE PEOPLE
WE WANT ACTION!

Following the old Hollywood belief that 'there's no such thing as bad publicity,' he fed the newspapers full accounts of the fighting between Nazis and Communists that occurred at almost every meeting. It worked – party recruitment soared.

BRAINWASHING ON A NATIONAL SCALE

He organised the party's election campaigns with ever increasing success. Above all he planned party rallies like theatrical productions with marching ranks of stormtroopers, torchlight parades, and cheering crowds.

GOEBBELS TAKES OVER

With the help of all this brilliantly organised propaganda, Hitler became Chancellor in 1933. He rewarded Goebbels by making him Reichsminister for Propaganda and Public Enlightenment. This meant that Goebbels had the media under his total command – all of it! Newspapers, magazines, radio, theatre, films, even sporting events, everything Germans saw, heard or read was pushing the Nazi Party line. It was brainwashing on a national scale.

POPULAR PRESS

The foreign press got particular attention. In London overseas journalists were lucky to get a few grudging words from some sniffy civil servant. In Berlin, everything was laid on.

A luxurious press centre, daily briefing meetings, guided tours – you could see everything the Nazis wanted you to see, learn everything they wanted you to know. (Ask any awkward questions though, and you soon found yourself on the first plane home.)

GOEBBELS'S GAMES

The Berlin Olympic Games of 1936 provided Goebbels with his greatest public relations success. Theatres and cinemas put on their best programmes and there were parties and receptions for the VIP visitors. Anti-Jewish propaganda was suspended for the duration of the Olympics. Goebbels even had the 'No Jews' signs taken off the park benches in case they made a bad impression...

GOEBBELS IN TROUBLE

Cinema and theatre were particularly important to Goebbels, and he took a keen interest in the career of a number of young actresses. His wife, Magda, turned a blind eye to most of her husband's affairs, but one became so serious it threatened the marriage. Goebbels fell madly in love with a beautiful Czech actress called Lydia Barova – so much so that he decided to divorce Magda and marry her. There was an enormous scandal. Himmler and Goering, Goebbels's rivals in the party, made sure that the story reached Hitler.

Adolf, who was very fond of Magda and the six Goebbels children, was shocked. Goebbels begged Hitler to allow the divorce and make him ambassador to Japan. Hitler sternly refused, and ordered him to end the affair. Goebbels obeyed and the lovely Lydia was sent home to Czechoslovakia in disgrace.

Goebbels's rivals all hoped this would be the end of his career, but Hitler knew he still needed his propaganda wizard.

CRYSTAL NIGHT

To restore his credibility with Hitler, Goebbels organised the infamous Crystal Night, the Night of the Broken Glass.

On November 9th 1938, in revenge for the assassination of a German diplomat in Paris, Goebbels's Propaganda Ministry organised 'spontaneous anti-Jewish demonstrations.' All over Germany, synagogues were attacked and Jewish stores were destroyed. Streets everywhere were filled with broken glass. The Jewish community was made to pay for the damage it had 'provoked'.

PROPAGANDA WAR

A year later Hitler invaded Poland and World War Two began.

Goebbels took little part in the war itself, staying at home to inspire the German people. This was easy enough at first, as Hitler provided apparently unending victories. It got harder when the tide of war turned against Germany. It became impossible when defeat became inevitable. No amount of propaganda could cheer up a starving country, flattened by Allied bombs.

THE LAST PUBLICITY STUNT

As the Allied armies closed in on Berlin, Goebbels urged Hitler not to surrender or try to escape. The Fuehrer must stay on in his underground Berchtesgarden bunker, and die there, so ending the Nazi legend in suitably dramatic style. Hitler, fearful of capture by the advancing Russians, agreed. On April 30th Hitler committed suicide, appointing Goebbels his successor.

It was a short-lived appointment. Next day, Goebbels decided to follow his Fuehrer. He urged his wife to escape with the children, but Magda, a devoted Nazi, insisted on staying. The six children, presumably, were given no choice. Their parents poisoned them that night at supper. Then Goebbels said his farewells, offered Magda his arm, and they went upstairs to the garden. A few minutes later a shot was heard. The SS guards hurried upstairs and found Magda poisoned and Goebbels shot through the head. According to instructions, they soaked the bodies with petrol and set fire to them.

Goebbels's body burned amidst the burning ruins of Berlin. It was a fitting end for a man who had used his talents to enable others to commit the most terrible crimes.

MOUNTBATTEN 1900-1979

There's a saying about being born with a silver spoon in your mouth – Mountbatten was born with an entire canteen of cutlery.

A descendant of the Emperor Charlemagne, and of most of the royal families of Europe and a cousin of the Queen, the tall, handsome Mountbatten was as well-connected as they come. It didn't exactly hold him back in his career.

YOUNG DICKIE

He was born Prince Louis of Battenberg, and he was a greatgrandchild of Queen Victoria, who came to his christening. (He knocked off her spectacles.) His father, although of German descent, had chosen to become a British naval officer. In those days most European royals were related, hence the connection with Queen Victoria.

PRINCE LOUIS OF BATTENBURG... A GREAT-GRANDCHILD
OF QUEEN VICTORIA...

...WHO CAME TO HIS CHRISTENING (HE KNOCKED OFF HER SPECTACLES).

The baby was christened Louis Francis Albert Victor Nicholas. Not surprisingly this soon got shortened first to Nicky, then finally to Dickie, the name used by family and friends for the rest of his long life.

Even as a child little Dickie Mountbatten travelled widely, regularly visiting his aristocratic relations in Germany and Russia. Like most upper-class kids he was sent away to boarding school at an early age. Unimpressed by his rank as a Serene Highness of Battenberg, the other kids nicknamed him 'Batter pudding'. Dickie was happy enough at this first school. He grew up a big, cheerful boy, adequate, but not outstanding, at both work and games.

OSBORNE AND DARTMOUTH

Dickie was determined to follow his father into the Navy, and in 1913 he arrived at Osborne Naval College. Although his father was now First Sea Lord, and he himself was of royal blood, he didn't get any privileges. At first he was badly teased, but it eventually died down especially after he fought, and beat, an older boy who was his chief tormentor. Things got difficult in 1914 when the First World War broke out. It was a bad time for anyone with a German name and the family name of 'Battenberg' was eventually anglicised to 'Mountbatten'. Young Dickie was heartbroken when his father was unfairly dismissed from his post as First Sea Lord. One day, he vowed, he'd take his father's place.

After Osborne, Dickie went on to Dartmouth Naval College. It was a tough and frantically busy life, everything done at the double, with frequent beatings for any serious offence.

DICKIE ON TOUR

Dickie survived it all, and joined the 'Lion', Admiral Beattie's flagship, as a midshipman in 1916. He spent the rest of the war on patrol, becoming a sub-lieutenant just as the war ended in 1918. After a spell at Cambridge to complete his education, Mountbatten joined his cousin, the Prince of Wales, on royal tours to Australia, New Zealand, and later India.

MOUNTBATTEN MARRIED

In 1922, he married Edwina Ashley, an immensely rich heiress. They'd met in London before he left for India and fallen madly in love. She came out to India to be with him, and they married soon after his return, leaving for a six month honeymoon in America, where they met Douglas Fairbanks and Charlie Chaplin. Restless, intolerant and pleasure-loving, Edwina proved a good match for Mountbatten. They remained devoted to each other, though not exclusively so, throughout a long and often stormy marriage.

BACK TO SEA

After the excitements of royal tours and a honeymoon, Mountbatten had to think about his naval career. For once his aristocratic connections looked like holding him back. Some of his superior officers were wary of him, fearing he might have got above himself, and be no better than a playboy. Mountbatten had to work hard to re-establish himself.

MOUNTBATTEN AT WAR

By the time war broke out in 1939, Mountbatten was captain of the newly-commissioned destroyer, 'Kelly.' The new ship seemed cursed by bad luck. She was badly damaged by a mine on an early voyage, damaged again by a collision with another vessel. Dashing into action in Norway, Kelly was badly torpedoed, and was towed home under enemy attack.

Repaired yet again, Kelly went back to sea, with Mountbatten as the leader of a small flotilla. In 1941 the flotilla was sent to reinforce the Mediterranean Fleet. After seeing a good deal of action, Kelly was finally sunk by German dive-bombers after an attack on an airfield. Mountbatten was picked up with the other survivors and flown home. (Mountbatten's friend Noel Coward used the story of the Kelly in his famous war-time film 'In Which We Serve' – with Noel himself playing Mountbatten.)

COMBINED OPERATIONS

So far Mountbatten's wartime career hadn't been an unqualified success. However he was to get another chance. Winston Churchill, who still had great faith in him, appointed him Chief of Command Operations, with promotion to Vice-Admiral. Mountbatten worked hard in the post, planning a successful raid on the German occupied French port of Saint Nazaire.

A later attack on Dieppe turned out to be a disaster, and Mountbatten got much of the blame. This wasn't entirely fair. The raid, insisted on by his superiors for propaganda reasons, was a bad idea from the beginning. 'Too big for a raid, too small for an invasion,' it should never have been attempted. Mountbatten simply did his best to carry out an impossible task. However, it taught the Allies valuable lessons about the difficulties of invasion – lessons that were put to good use on D-Day.

By now America was in the war, and Mountbatten was involved in early planning for the invasion. He forged valuable links with General Eisenhower, and later with President Roosevelt. He got on well with Americans, who were more ready to accept his flamboyant nature, and were secretly impressed by his royal connections.

SUPREME COMMAND

In 1943 Mountbatten got another extraordinary promotion. In Asia the war against the Japanese was going badly. Churchill decided an energetic new supreme commander was needed. He suggested Mountbatten, and Roosevelt agreed.

Mountbatten spent the next two years commanding the long and difficult re-conquest of Burma and Singapore. It was as much a diplomatic as a military task, involving cooperation with American, Indian and Chinese troops, and their rival commanders.

Mountbatten put new life into the campaign, raising the morale of the troops, insisting it was possible to fight on through the monsoon season. He cemented good relations with the touchy Indian leaders, and with China's General Chiang Kai-shek. It was a long hard struggle, but eventually the Japanese were driven back. The dropping of the atom bomb put the finishing touches to Japanese defeat. On September 12th 1945 in Singapore, Mountbatten accepted the final surrender of Japanese forces in South-East Asia.

MOUNTBATTEN INSISTED IT WAS POSSIBLE TO FIGHT ON THROUGH THE MONSOON SEASON.

POST WAR

Some wartime personalities fade away when the war is over – but not Mountbatten. Created Earl Mountbatten of Burma, he was sent to India as the last viceroy, presiding over India's difficult path to independence. (Edwina went with him and formed a very close friendship with Indian Prime Minister Nehru.)

His royal connections went up another notch when his favourite nephew, Philip, married Princess Elizabeth, England's future queen. After India, Mountbatten returned to the Navy, and fulfilled his ambition of following his father in the post of First Sea Lord. Finally he became chief of the defence staff.

His later years were touched with scandal when the press, including 'Private Eye', accused him of being gay in his younger days. Mountbatten, who'd always prided himself on being something of a ladies man, was both amazed and amused.

MOUNTBATTEN'S END

Mountbatten's long and colourful life had a dramatic finish. In August 1979, old but still active, and retired from all his great offices, he was enjoying a family holiday at Classiebawn Castle in Ireland. He set out for a boat trip with a group of family friends. As the boat passed the harbour wall it blew up. The IRA had planted a fifty-pound bomb. Mountbatten was killed instantly.

THE AMAZING MOUNTBATTEN

Incredibly privileged from birth, Mountbatten had greatness almost thrust upon him. He had good looks, energy, courage, tremendous charm, and an almost child-like vanity. He was promoted – many said over-promoted – to high rank at an amazingly early age. It's natural to suspect that his royal connections had a lot to do with his rapid rise.

Mountbatten had his faults and his failures, and he had many critics. Some of their criticisms were deserved. Brave and daring, he was often rash and reckless, and the ships he commanded usually ended up in trouble.

But it's also true that many of the attacks on Mountbatten stemmed from envy. After all, when someone's tall and handsome, rich and royal, and the youngest admiral in the Navy, it's almost impossible not to envy them.

Mountbatten worked hard at the many important posts that he filled, often working for 12 or 14 hours a day. His successes far outnumbered his failures.

Born to the highest rank, rich enough never to have to work, Mountbatten devoted his life to the service of his country. He always did his absolute best – and you can't ask more than that.

DE GAULLE 1890–1970

When France was decisively defeated by Germany in 1940, sensible soldiers accepted the facts and signed an armistice.

Charles de Gaulle refused to recognise reality – and went on to help liberate his beloved country and become its President. It just goes to show, common sense isn't everything...

LITTLE CHARLIE

Charles de Gaulle was born in Lille in 1890 into a cultured upper-class French family. His father was a professor of philosophy. As a child de Gaulle was a little devil, full of tricks and mischief, with a passion for toy soldiers, with which he and his brothers fought miniature wars. Not surprisingly his ambition was to join the Army.

Little Charles grew up to be an exceptionally tall young man. He was nicknamed 'The Asparagus' after the tall thin plant.

At twenty-one he entered the famous French Military Academy at Saint Cyr.

CHARLIE'S WAR (I)

Graduating with honours, Charles joined the Army in 1913 as a second-lieutenant. He was a full lieutenant by the time war broke out in 1914.

A keen and capable soldier, de Gaulle saw plenty of action. He was wounded twice in the first two years of the war, and promoted to captain. Then, in 1916, he was wounded again in the fierce fighting around Verdun. He was scooped up by the Germans and taken to a prison camp hospital in Germany. As soon as he recovered he was sent to a prisoner of war camp.

DE GAULLE WAS JUST TOO TALL TO MISS!

De Gaulle made no less than five attempts to escape but he was recaptured almost immediately each time. He was just too tall to miss! He spent the last two years of the war in captivity, until he was freed by the French victory in 1918.

BETWEEN WARS

Promoted to commandant, the released de Gaulle went back to Saint Cyr as professor of history. He saw more action in 1921 when the French sent a Military Mission to help Poland resist the Russian Bolsheviks.

Their follwed more lecturing at Saint Cyr, followed by a course at the Staff College in Paris. De Gaulle was developing strategic theories of his own by now. The orthodox idea of the time was that of static defence. You chose your battlefield carefully, fortified it, and lured the enemy on to inevitable defeat. De Gaulle preferred more flexible tactics, based on speed and freedom of movement.

DE GAULLE ABROAD

Now a rising young officer, de Gaulle soon reached the rank of major. He served in the French Army of Occupation in the Rhineland, and then on a special government commission, visiting Egypt, Iran, Iraq, and Syria.

Back in France, de Gaulle, now a lieutenant-colonel, served on the Defence Council. He continued to write books urging the creating of a professional, modern mechanised army.

No-one in France took any notice – but the books were studied with interest in a now rearming Germany...

TROUBLE AHEAD

In 1937 de Gaulle was placed in command of a regiment of tanks at Metz in the Rhineland. He was all too aware of the frantic rearmament going on over the border in Germany. France meanwhile clung to the old static defence idea, relying on the fortified Maginot Line. By now Germany had ten armoured divisions. France had four. When war broke out in 1939, German Panzer Divisions swept through Poland. De Gaulle drew up a memo outlining the dangers, sending it to his superior officers and to the Government. Still no one took any notice. Soon the German Panzers were sweeping through France as well.

DE GAULLE'S WAR (II)

De Gaulle was promoted to brigadier-general and his tanks took part in the unsuccessful attempt to hold back the enemy, mounting one of the strongest counter-attacks of the brief campaign.

Then he was sent for by the French Prime Minister, Reynaud, and appointed under-secretary for War. Sent on a special mission to London, de Gaulle urged a union of France and Britain so that the two countries could fight on together. But when he returned to France he found that Reynaud had resigned, and that his successor, Marshal Petain, was already negotiating a surrender. Seeing that all was lost, de Gaulle flew back to Britain.

THE FREE FRENCHMAN

Up to now, de Gaulle had always avoided politics, but now he had no choice. Filled with a sense of mission, de Gaulle became convinced that he alone could save France. Appointing himself leader of the Free French in exile, de Gaulle appealed to all French forces on British territory to rally to the cause. He broadcast to France from London, promising to carry on the fight.

DE GAULLE BROADCAST TO FRANCE FROM LONDON...

In France, the new Vichy government, under German pressure, court-martialled him in his absence and sentenced him to death.

DE GAULLE IN EXILE

De Gaulle was in a difficult position in the years that followed. His country had been defeated, and most of it had surrendered. The self-proclaimed leader of a scattered band of exiles, he was little more than an Allied hanger-on.

De Gaulle refused to admit it for one moment. Tall and dignified, he demanded to be treated as an equal. 'I am France,' he announced – and by now he believed it. He spent much of the time quarrelling with his British and American allies.

RETURN IN TRIUMPH

The Allies tried to keep him out of things when they could. They didn't even tell him about their invasion of the French territories of North Africa until it was well under way.

In 1943 de Gaulle became head of the French Committee of National Liberation, based in Algiers, and this became the basis of a provisional government for France. In 1944 de Gaulle and his Free French troops entered Paris, in the wake of the Allied armies. By now de Gaulle had become the living symbol of French resistance. He received a rapturous reception, and his administration was formally recognised by the Allies.

PRESIDENT DE GAULLE

With no more Germans to fight, de Gaulle naturally started quarrelling with his own side. In 1946, he resigned in a huff and went off to sulk in his home in Colombey-les-Deux-Eglises.

He didn't stay away for long. He played a prominent part in the resolution of France's Algerian crisis in 1958 and in 1959 he became President of the Republic.

(Madame de Gaulle later caused a minor crisis on a visit to England. Asked by journalists what she truly valued in life, she astonished them by replying, 'All I want is a penis.' Fortunately someone realised what she was trying to say. It was 'All I want is happiness' – in a strong French accent!)

THE LEGEND OF DE GAULLE

During the war and afterwards, de Gaulle was a towering figure in French politics, the symbol of his country. When he died in 1970, President Pompidou announced that 'France was widowed.'

Although de Gaulle began as a patriotic soldier with no interest in politics, fate forced him into a political role. He became convinced that he was the destined saviour of France. De Gaulle's growing belief in his own legend made him arrogant and intolerant, unable to put up with any opposition, especially from those on his own side. These qualities made him almost impossible to work with, as big a trial to his allies as to his enemies.

On the other hand, it was exactly this unwavering confidence in his destiny that enabled him, in 1940, to defy the Nazis – and the facts – and insist that one day France would be free. 'I am France!' General de Gaulle once said. For a time at least, it was true.

MACARTHUR 1880–1964

Generals are important people – but few of them rise to be emperors. Tall, handsome and highly charismatic, MacArthur enjoyed a spectacular rise – which ended in a dramatic fall.

MAC'S WAR (I)

Son of a distinguished officer who'd fought in the American Civil War, Douglas MacArthur was always destined to be a soldier. He graduated from West Point in 1903, head of his class.

By the time America entered the war, MacArthur was a colonel. He fought in France in the bloody battle of the Marne. Promoted to brigadier general, MacArthur was given command of the 42nd Division. He was the youngest divisional commander of the war, and was described as America's best front-line general.

BETWEEN THE WARS

After the war MacArthur became Chief of the General Staff, reorganising the Army. In 1935 he was sent to the Philippines to help them prepare for independence. He was given command of the tiny Commonwealth Army. Enjoying his own importance, MacArthur took the imposing title of Field Marshal, designing himself a snappy sharkskin uniform.

MACARTHUR DESIGNED HIMSELF A
SPECIAL SHARKSKIN UNIFORM

MAC'S WAR (II)

Immediately before the Second World War, MacArthur was
appointed commander of US Army forces in the Far East. After
their attack on Pearl Harbour on December 7th 1941, the
Japanese invaded the Philippines in force. With an army of
American and Filipino troops, MacArthur fought a stubborn
defensive action. His troops fought to hold the islands of Bataan
and Corregidor against impossible odds. In the end they were
overwhelmed.

MAC'S PROMISE

MacArthur himself was ordered to retreat to Australia. After
giving his famous pledge, 'I shall return', he arrived in Australia
in 1942. He was appointed Supreme Allied Commander in the
South West Pacific.

Faced with innumerable Japanese-occupied islands, MacArthur
devised the policy of 'island hopping', by-passing strongly held
islands to capture smaller and weaker ones, cutting Japanese

communications, and moving ever closer to Japan.

MACARTHUR'S VICTORY

By spring 1944, New Guinea and the Solomon Islands had been recaptured. In February 1945 the Americans re-captured Manila. Keeping his promise, MacArthur had returned to the Philippines.

Promoted to Supreme Commander of US Forces in the Pacific, MacArthur went on to capture Iwo Jima and invade Okinawa, two islands very close to Japan. The dropping of atomic bombs on Hiroshima and Nagasaki brought war with Japan to an end. On the 2nd of September 1945, MacArthur accepted the Japanese surrender.

BIG MAC

As Supreme Commander for the Allied Powers, MacArthur became total and absolute ruler of Japan. Respecting Japanese traditions, he allowed the Emperor of Japan to keep his throne – but everyone knew who was the real emperor.

Over the next six years, MacArthur totally remodelled Japanese society, replacing old feudal traditions with democratic ideas. He introduced land reforms and health and welfare systems. (He horrified the Japanese by introducing rights for women.)

BACK TO WAR

It was the Korean war that brought Douglas MacArthur's career to a bitter end. When war broke out in 1950, he was appointed Commander of United Nations troops in Korea. The UN forces were defending South Korea from the attacks of North Korea – but everyone knew that the real enemy was communist China. Frustrated by fighting a war at one remove, MacArthur publicly urged the use of the atomic bomb against China.

US President Harry Truman wanted to contain the Korean war, not expand it into World War Three. He told MacArthur to shut up. MacArthur refused. He went on urging the use of the bomb.

By this time MacArthur had enormous prestige and influence – and the arrogance to go with it. He thought he was untouchable. To everyone's astonishment, especially MacArthur's, Truman fired him. The American Army was stunned by MacArthur's dismissal. They were even more amazed when the previously fine weather suddenly changed to gale force winds and snowstorms. 'Say,' said a worried soldier, 'maybe he is God after all!'

' MACARTHUR HAS BEEN DISMISSED – THERE WILL NOW BE GALES, SNOWSTORMS AND PLAGUES OF LITTLE FROGS ... '

HOME AT LAST

MacArthur received a hero's welcome when he returned to America. He made a farewell speech to the Senate, saying: 'Old soldiers never die, they only fade away.'

Not wanting to fade away just yet, MacArthur tried to get himself nominated for the presidency, hoping, no doubt, to show Truman who was boss. The attempt didn't succeed.

Instead of being President, MacArthur became chairman of the board of the huge Rand Corporation. In 1961 he went back to his beloved Philippines, to help celebrate the 50th anniversary of independence. He died in 1964, eighty-four years old.

SUMMING UP

MacArthur was undoubtedly one of America's greatest generals. In the Pacific he fought an incredibly tough and complex campaign, surviving defeat and turning it into victory.

He was often accused of arrogance, but those close to him spoke of unfailing courtesy and kindness.

MacArthur had his faults but he was a great man and a great soldier. If his military career ended unhappily, it was sacrificed for an important principle.

In a democracy, it's the elected politicians, not the soldiers who make the decisions...

PATTON 1885-1945

Different generals have differing attitudes to war. Eisenhower hated it. Montgomery saw it as a job, to be carried out efficiently and economically. Patton loved it. 'Compared to war, all other human endeavours sink into insignificance. God, how I love it!'

A colourful character who made a habit of wearing a pair of ivory-handled six guns, Patton was known to his troops as 'Old Blood-and-Guts.'

'OLD BLOOD-AND-GUTS'

SOLDIER GEORGE

George Smith Patton was born in 1885 in San Gabriel California into a rich family with a tradition of army service. He spent a year at the Virginia Military Academy, going on to West Point in 1904. He suffered from dyslexia, and he didn't graduate until 1909, when he was posted to a cavalry regiment. A keen athlete, Patton competed in the Pentathlon in the 1912 Olympic Games – the first American ever.

GEORGE'S WAR (I)

Patton didn't lose any time getting into action. Before America entered the war he served in the Mexican Punitive Expedition as aide to General 'Black Jack' Pershing. He later accompanied Pershing to France. By 1918 he was commanding a tank brigade in the Argonne offensive. He was wounded in action, and won the Distinguished Service Cross.

BETWEEN THE WARS

Promoted to major in 1919, Patton was given command of a tank battalion, and later served in the office of the chief of cavalry. He attended the Cavalry School, the General Staff School and the Army War College.

GEORGE'S WAR (II)

After time spent in Washington, planning the Allied invasion of North Africa, Patton finally got back into action in 1942, commanding the Allied task force which landed in North Africa.

Things in North Africa got off to a very bad start. Inexperienced American troops were badly hammered by Rommel's Afrika Korps at the Battle of Kasserine Pass. Morale was at rock bottom. Patton's first task was to put some heart into his discouraged troops. His tough, flamboyant personality was tailor-made for the job. No more retreats, no more defeats, said Patton, and his soldiers believed him. Together with Monty's

Desert Rats, they drove Rommel out of North Africa.

PATTON STORMS AHEAD

Promoted to lieutenant general, Patton was given command of the US Seventh Army in the invasion of Sicily. His army's task was to support Monty's Eighth Army in its drive for Messina. But Patton wasn't the sort of man to be satisfied with a supporting role. When the more cautious Monty got bogged down, Patton raced ahead and captured the important port of Palermo. Then he swung east and reached Messina before the Eighth Army.

Monty was far from pleased, saying Patton had exceeded his orders and acted with dangerous rashness. All perfectly true — but you can't argue with success.

PATTON IN DISGRACE

Patton's rashness was to land him in serious trouble. Visiting badly-wounded troops in a hospital behind the lines, Patton came across an apparently unwounded soldier, and asked him why he was there. The confused and delirious soldier said he just couldn't take it any more. Patton slapped him and called him a coward.

When the story got out there was a world-wide storm of protest. To make matters worse, it emerged that the soldier was suffering from malaria, and had every right to be in hospital.

Patton's supreme commander, the usually mild-mannered Eisenhower, was furious. Patton was severely reprimanded. He was ordered to apologise to the soldier personally, and to the

Army at large. Worst of all, when the Allies invaded Italy, Patton was left behind in Sicily on occupation duties. To the glory-loving Patton, it was the worst punishment of all.

FOOLING HITLER

But good fighting generals are always in short supply. Patton was just too good to waste. Ike sent him to England, where the D-Day invasion was being prepared. Patton became the centre of an extraordinary deception. The Allies invented a totally fictitious army group, announcing that Patton was to be in command. The group was to suppose to invade the area around Calais. Hitler was fooled and kept a large part of his army in the wrong place.

D-DAY AND AFTER

After the Normandy invasion, Patton commanded the US Third Army. In typical Patton style, his tanks broke out of Avranches, dashed towards the Loire – and ground to a halt when he ran out of supplies. Patton grumbled that if they'd given him extra supplies instead of that old slowcoach Montgomery, he would have reached Germany and shortened the war!

But when the Germans made a sudden comeback, taking the Allies by surprise and driving them back in the battle of the Bulge, Patton's dash and daring was exactly what was needed. He swung his army round to the North with astonishing speed, and drove into the Germans southern flank, smashing their attack.

ON TO VICTORY

In the last year of the war, Patton's Third Army raced to the Rhine, crossed into Germany, and then sped clear across Bavaria to Czechoslovakia, moving further and faster than any other Allied commander. It could have been a disaster, as his flanks were left totally unprotected, but somehow Patton pulled it off.

BACK IN TROUBLE

After the war, Patton's outspoken rashness soon got him in trouble again. He distrusted America's Russian allies, and saw their presence in Europe as a menace. Patton said publicly and out loud that the American tanks should just keep rolling until they reached Moscow.

END OF A SOLDIER

It was an attitude that didn't go down too well with Patton's superiors. They took the Third Army away from him, before he could take off towards Moscow with it, and put him in command of the Fifteenth Army, a force which existed largely on paper.

It's hard to know what would have become of Patton. Peace just didn't suit him. In December 1945, Fate suddenly solved the problem. Patton was involved in a major traffic accident. His car crashed and he suffered a broken neck, dying in hospital in Heidelberg some days later.

'BLOOD-AND-GUTS' AND GLORY

Patton may have lacked the vision for really high command, but as a commander on the battlefield he was unequalled for skill and daring. The truth is that Patton was born out of his time. He belonged in a more primitive age, when a love of war was nothing to be ashamed of. The title of the Hollywood film about Patton sums it up very well.

It was called 'Lust for Glory'...

ANNE FRANK 1929-1945

We've been talking mainly about the VIPs of World War Two — but war touches the lives of millions of ordinary people, often with tragic results. This is especially true of Anne Frank.

YOUNG ANNE

Anne Frank was born in Frankfurt-am-Main in 1929. She was the daughter of Otto Frank, a German Jewish businessman. When Anne was still a toddler the Nazis came to power in Germany, and began their ever-increasing persecution of the Jews. In 1933 Otto Frank moved his business and his family to the Netherlands.

ANNE FRANK

Anne spent her early years in Amsterdam, attending school, making friends, enjoying a normal happy childhood. Tragically, Otto Frank hadn't moved far enough. War broke out in 1939, and by 1941 the Nazis had occupied the Netherlands.

OCCUPATION

The Frank family found their lives more and more restricted. Like all other Jews, they had a curfew, cinemas and swimming baths were barred to them and they had to wear a yellow star. Jews began receiving instructions to report to transit camps. From there trains took them away. Nobody ever came back.

OTTO'S PLAN

Otto Frank conceived a daring plan. He was a spice importer and his business premises included a warehouse. He sealed off part of the warehouse as a secret annexe, converting it into a hidden apartment for himself and his family. Mr and Mrs Frank and their two daughters moved into the secret annexe on July 9th, 1942. Generously, they gave shelter to another family, Mr and Mrs van Daan and their son Peter, and to an elderly dentist.

IN HIDING

The Franks and their friends lived in the secret apartment for two whole years. Non-Jewish Dutch employees of Otto Frank risked their lives to bring them food. Unable to go out, they lived in overcrowded, cramped conditions, in daily fear of discovery. German soldiers came to look for them, the police searched the premises after an attempted burglary, but the Franks and their friends were still not found. When they heard of the Allied landings in France in 1944, their hopes of freedom rose.

ANNE'S DIARY

To help pass the time, Anne kept a diary. In it she put all the details and petty problems of their daily life, all her hopes and fears, and her longing for a better future.

At fourteen Anne was on the verge of womanhood. She and young Peter van Daan fell in love. It was a love without a future. On August 4th 1944 the fugitives were betrayed by an unknown informer. The Gestapo arrived at the warehouse and took them away to different concentration camps. Otto Frank was the only one of his family to survive. Anne's mother died in Ravensbruck, Anne and her sister died of typhus in Belsen. Anne was brave and uncomplaining to the last. The van Daans and the old dentist all died in concentration camps as well.

IMMORTAL ANNE

After the war Otto Frank came back to the warehouse. One of his employees had found Anne's diary, lying forgotten in a corner, after the family's arrest. The employee gave the diary to Otto who published it in 1947. 'The Diary of Anne Frank' became a world bestseller, translated into thirty languages.

It was made into a film, a stage play and a television serial. The warehouse where Anne hid is now a museum. Every year, thousands of young people come to pay tribute to her memory. An intelligent, attractive young girl, just beginning her life. One victim, amongst six million, who will never be forgotten.

LENI RIEFENSTAHL 1902–

The life of Leni Riefenstahl raises some interesting artistic questions. No one denies that Leni made wonderful movies. The trouble is, she made the best of them to glorify Adolf Hitler.

LENI ON STAGE

Leni Riefenstahl was born in Berlin in 1902. She began her career as a dancer, studying at the Berlin School of Crafts. Later she appeared with the Russian ballet, and worked for the famous director, Max Reinhardt. In the twenties she enjoyed a successful career, first as a dancer, later as an actress.

LENI RIEFENSTAHL

LENI ON FILM

Leni became interested in films by appearing in them. She appeared in 'The Holy Mountain' which was a film with an Alpine background, and a maritime drama called 'SOS Iceberg'. In 1931 she set up her own film company. 'The Blue Light', a film she wrote, directed and starred in – move over, Orson Welles – won a prize at Venice in 1932.

PROPAGANDA LENI

Her success had attracted the attention of the Nazi Party and Goebbels commissioned her to make a propaganda movie, 'Victory of Faith'. It isn't one of her best works, possibly because she hated working with Goebbels so much that she had a nervous breakdown – which at least shows good taste.

ADOLF INTERVENES

In 1934 however, Hitler personally persuaded her to make a film of the Nazi Party's Nuremburg Rally. The resulting film, 'Triumph of the Will', is an undoubted masterpiece. Unfortunately, it's a masterpiece of Nazi propaganda, packed with marching stormtroopers, cheering crowds, and thrilling torchlight rallies. Brilliantly shot, it's powerful enough to make the most ardent liberal jump up and start shouting 'Sieg Heil!' Hitler, well aware of the power of the new medium, used the movie to promote and glorify the Nazi Party.

LENI'S OLYMPICS

Leni's next great film had a similar motive, though it was somewhat better disguised. In 1938 she produced another Nazi masterpiece, 'Olympia', a documentary about the 1936 Olympics.

It was premiered on Hitler's birthday, with Adolf himself in the audience, and it later won a prize at Venice. This film, too, is a stunning and astonishing achievement. It conveys all the beauty and excitement of the Olympic Games. But it also conveys, as Adolf intended, the power and prestige of the new Third Reich.

POST-WAR BLUES

After the Third Reich finally collapsed, Leni fled to France, where she was arrested and imprisoned for her part in the Nazi propaganda machine. However she was soon released – no one seemed very clear about what crime she was supposed to have committed.

Leni herself always protested her innocence: she knew nothing of politics, nothing about the persecution of the Jews, and despite all the rumours, she and Adolf were just good friends. As time went by the memories of her Nazi associations have faded and her status as a film maker has been restored. In 1948 the Olympic committee gave her an award for the 'Olympia' film.

Leni Riefenstahl's line about just being an innocent unpolitical artist doesn't really carry conviction. Take another look at all those marching SS men in 'Triumph of the Will'. Good film-maker as she was, Leni Riefenstahl can't escape the taint of the ghastly regime she served so well.

HIMMLER 1900-1945

When it comes to choosing the nastiest Nazi, Himmler has to be one of the leading nominees. Small, pale and bespectacled, one of nature's filing-clerks, he was a monster disguised as a nerd.

A MONSTER DISGUISED
AS A NERD

YOUNG HEINRICH

Heinrich Himmler was born in Munich in 1900, the son of a schoolmaster. He served briefly in World War One as a cadet-clerk, then went on to Munich Technical College where he studied agriculture. An early Nazi Party member, he became its business manager and rose to be a gauleiter, or district leader, in Bavaria. He married in 1928, and became a part-time chicken farmer.

HIMMLER TRIED TO BECOME A CHICKEN FARMER

HIMMLER'S SS

In 1929, Hitler appointed Himmler head of his personal bodyguard, the black-uniformed SS. Little Heinrich was about to become a big man. He built up the SS to an immense organisation with a membership of over 50,000. He organised the Gestapo, the secret state police, whose files had all the dirt on everyone, including his fellow Nazi leaders.

When the brown-shirted SA, the rank-and-file stormtroopers, began getting above themselves, Himmler organised the 'Night of the Long Knives,' the bloodbath that disposed of them. In 1936 Hitler appointed Himmler Reichsfuehrer SS. Himmler was now in control of both the SS and the Gestapo. Next to Hitler, he was the most powerful man in Germany.

In 1939, with the outbreak of war, Himmler took on the task of eliminating Jews, Poles, gypsies, Russians, Czechs, and anyone else Hitler considered undesirable. He set up extermination camps and instituted a policy of mass slaughter. It was deliberate, organised genocide, the greatest crime in human history.

AFTER THE PLOT

The generals' unsuccessful attempt to assassinate Hitler in 1944 consolidated Himmler's power. Now he was the only one the paranoid Hitler trusted, his 'faithful Heinrich'.

The worse the situation in Germany became, the greater grew Himmler's influence. He even persuaded Hitler to give him an army to command. Since Himmler had no military experience whatever, the result was total disaster. Soldiers' lives were wasted, and the German Army retreated still faster before the advancing Russians.

HIMMLER'S END

By now even Himmler realised the end was near, and he began making peace overtures to the Allies. When the news reached the Fuehrer's bunker, Hitler was furious. He stripped Himmler of all his state offices and ordered his arrest.

After the German surrender, Himmler tried to escape in disguise. He shaved off his moustache, put on an eye-patch, and took the uniform and papers of an ex-policeman called Hitzinger. He was captured just outside Bremen by British troops, and the briefest interrogation penetrated his feeble disguise. On May 23rd 1945 Himmler swallowed a hidden cyanide capsule and died, escaping certain execution at Nuremburg.

MAD AND BAD

Himmler was a mystic as well as a murderer, believing in every sort of psychic nonsense, and in all the crackpot theories about the superiority of the Aryan race. To him, the SS weren't just a gang of murderous thugs, they were a mystic order of Teutonic knights, with secret oaths and ceremonies. No doubt about it, Heinrich Himmler was ghastly beyond belief.

TOJO 1884–1948

GENERAL TOJO

Tojo began his career as a military police chief in the Japanese Army. By 1935 he was Chief of Staff, and in 1938 he became Deputy War Minister. Japan had long been concerned about America's increasing influence in the pacific. Tojo, who was a member of an extreme militarist group called Toseiha, regarded war with America as both necessary and inevitable. He was looking forward to it.

GENERAL HIDEKI TOJO

PRIME MINISTER TOJO

General Tojo became Prime Minister in 1941. He soon appointed himself Chief of Staff as well, and every important office in Japan came under his command. Even now not everyone in Japan wanted war. The Emperor Hirohito was anxious for peace, and Yamamoto, Japan's greatest admiral,

154

doubted if Japan could ever defeat a country with America's enormous resources.

Tojo, however, urged a surprise attack on Pearl Harbour, and he got his way. The attack was treacherously carried out – at a time when Japanese representatives were still engaged in treaty negotiations in America.

TOJO'S END

As the war began to go badly for Japan, Tojo lost influence. In 1944 he was forced to resign as Prime Minister. When the Americans entered Tokyo in 1945, Tojo made an unsuccessful attempt to commit suicide. He was tried as a war criminal, and executed in 1948.

If you think about it, we Europeans owe Tojo something of a debt. Without the attack on Pearl Harbour, America might never have entered the war – and the end result might have turned out to be very different.

HANNAH REITSCH 1912-1979

One of the better side-effects of both world wars was the inevitable liberation of women as they took over jobs once reserved for men. Hannah Reitsch didn't need any liberating...

TEST PILOT HANNAH

Hannah was born in Silesia in 1912, the daughter of an ophthalmologist. Fascinated by flying from the very beginning, she determined to become a pilot. It was no job for a lady in those days, but the determined Hannah achieved it against all opposition. Her original plan was to be a missionary flying doctor, but she abandoned the idea to become a professional pilot. Soon she was one of Germany's leading stunt flyers. In 1937 General Udet appointed her a test pilot for the Luftwaffe.

HANNAH AT WAR

Hannah served with the Luftwaffe throughout the war. She even test-piloted the experimental VI rocket craft, before it was decided to turn it into an unmanned robot bomb. She was the only woman to earn the Iron Cross (first and second class).

HANNAH AND HITLER

Hannah's real claim to fame came at the very end of the war. On April 26th 1945 she flew General von Greim into Hitler's bunker, which was already under heavy fire from Allied guns. She stayed in the beleaguered bunker for three days, while von

Greim conferred with Hitler. Hannah, a dedicated Nazi, begged Hitler to let her stay and die with him. Hitler however ordered her to fly von Greim, now the new head of the Luftwaffe, out again. Avoiding Russian anti-aircraft guns, Hannah obeyed. Escaping from Berlin, she was captured by the Americans. A year later they let her go, and Hannah got on with her career as an international test pilot.

HESS 1894-1987

Even for a Nazi leader, Hess was undeniably weird. His career, and his life, ended in mysteries that have never been explained.

HESS WAS UNDENIABLY WEIRD (LIKE THIS CARTOON)

RELIABLE RUDOLPH

Rudolph Hess served in the same regiment as Hitler in World War One. They shared a cell in Landsberg Fortress after Hitler's failed Munich coup. When they got out of jail, Hess became Hitler's private secretary. He soon rose to high office in the Nazi Party, ending up as Deputy Fuehrer.

HESS TAKES FLIGHT

On May 10th 1941, Hess flew from Germany to Scotland, landing by parachute and breaking his ankle. He was captured by a farmer with a pitchfork and taken first to hospital and later to the Tower of London. Hess explained that he had come to make peace. Britain and Germany must form an alliance against the Russians. He was hurt and astonished when no one took him seriously. Hitler disowned him, saying he was raving mad.

HESS FLEW TO SCOTLAND AND WAS CAPTURED
BY A FARMER WITH A PITCHFORK

PRISONER HESS

Hess stayed in the Tower until 1946, when he was taken to Nuremburg, to stand trial with the other surviving Nazi leaders. At his trial he was wide-eyed and vacant, answering all questions with, 'I don't remember.' He was found guilty of war crimes and sentenced to life imprisonment. Hess stayed in Spandau prison until his suicide in 1987. Even then the mystery wasn't over. There's a rumour that Hess was murdered, another that the Spandau prisoner wasn't Hess at all. There's even a theory that Hess's peace mission was official. Only Adolf Hitler and his aide, the famously missing Martin Bormann, knew the truth – and Adolf's dead and Bormann can't be found...

QUISLING 1887–1945

Usually it's an honour to have your name become part of the language – but there are exceptions...

QUISLING'S CAREER

Vidkun Quisling was born in Norway in 1887. As a young man he worked for Nansen, the famous polar explorer, and for the United Nations in Russia. He returned to Norway in 1929 and entered politics as an anti-communist candidate, becoming Foreign Minister in 1931. In 1933 he founded the Norwegian Fascist Party.

QUISLING'S FRIENDS

In 1939 Quisling sent Adolf a message, saying Britain was about to occupy Norway, and Hitler had better get in first.

When the Germans invaded Norway in 1940, Quisling proclaimed himself Prime Minister. Even the occupying Germans weren't all that keen on the idea. They noticed that Quisling's fellow Norwegians didn't want to have anything to do with him.

HELP FROM HITLER

Eventually Adolf gave Quisling his support, and for a time the Norwegian Fascist Party was the only legal one. In 1942, Hitler confirmed Quisling as Prime Minister. In fact he was little more than a puppet. The real power was in the hands of Josef Terboven, Reich Commissioner for Norway. Always a nasty piece of work, Quisling used his bit of power to punish his political opponents.

END OF A TRAITOR

Shortly after Germany's surrender in 1945, Vidkun Quisling was arrested. Tried as a traitor by the new Norwegian Government he was sentenced to death and shot in Oslo. Since then Quisling's name simply means 'traitor and collaborator' in any language. It's a rotten way to be remembered...

ODETTE 1912-1995

In the early years of World War Two, nearly all Europe was under Nazi occupation. Winston Churchill issued a typically inspiring call for Resistance; 'Set Europe ablaze!'

The organisation given this task was the Special Operations Executive, SOE for short. Odette Sansom was one of its agents.

SOE

In the spring of 1942, a young Frenchwoman, married to an Englishman and living in England, heard an official radio appeal for photographs of the French coastline. She looked out some old holiday snaps and sent them to the War Office. Some days later she was invited for a personal interview – and asked if she'd be willing to go into German-occupied France as an agent of SOE.

ODETTE

Astonished as she was, Odette felt it was her duty to accept. After basic training in codes, secret messages, and the use of firearms and explosives, she was given a cover story, the code name Lise, and sent off to France.

RESISTANCE AND BETRAYAL

Odette landed at night from a fishing boat near Cassis in the South of France. She worked for the Resistance for a year. Her superior officer was Captain Peter Churchill, code name Raoul. They sent vital Marseilles harbour plans to England, and arranged for arms supplies to be dropped to the French Resistance. Then they were betrayed, arrested and taken to Fresnes prison.

GESTAPO

What happens next is told in Odette's George Cross citation. 'The Gestapo were most determined to discover the whereabouts of the radio operator and of another British officer...Mrs Sansom was the only person who knew of their whereabouts. The Gestapo tortured her most brutally to try and make her give away this information. They seared her back with a red-hot iron, and when that failed they pulled out all her toenails. Mrs Sansom, however, continually refused to speak and by her bravery and determination she not only saved the lives of the two officers but also enabled them to carry on their most valuable work.'

RAVENSBRUCK

Unable to get anything out of Odette, the Gestapo sentenced her to death. But the sentence was not carried out. Instead she was sent to the women's concentration camp at Ravensbruck. There she survived, under brutal and harsh conditions, for two years.

LIBERATION

Odette's life was saved by her cover story. She and Captain Churchill had agreed to tell the Gestapo that they were married. Peter Churchill was related to the famous Winston, and he had been sent to a special camp for potentially valuable hostages.

The Churchill name protected Odette too. With the war nearly over and the Americans nearing Ravensbruck, the camp commandant himself drove her to the American lines. Trying to ingratiate himself with the Americans, he insisted Odette was 'Frau Churchill, a relative of the British Prime Minister.'

AN ORDINARY WOMAN

Odette was awarded the George Cross for her heroism. She and Peter Churchill eventually married so their cover story came true. A best-selling book, 'Odette', was written about her.

In 1950, her story was told in a Royal Command Performance film. Odette was rather embarrassed by all the publicity. She always insisted that she was 'a very ordinary woman.'

VERA LYNN 1919 -

Sometimes just one person can become a symbol for a nation. Winston Churchill was one and so was General de Gaulle. And so, in her own way, was a singer called Vera Lynn...

LITTLE VERA

Vera Lynn was born in London's East End, just after the First World War, entering show business at a very early age. She was dancing on stage by the time she was eleven. At fourteen she was leading her own dance troupe.

VERA SINGS

She began her career as a singer in the pubs and clubs of the East End. Very soon she moved on to greater things. She sang with the Joe Loss Band, Ambrose and his Orchestra, and the pianist Charlie Kunz – great names in the thirties and forties.

THE FORCE'S SWEETHEART

During the war Vera Lynn was a national institution. Radio was really big in those days and she sang on a programme aimed at servicemen. It was called 'Sincerely Yours'.

♪ YOU'LL HEAR THIS SONG AGAIN,
DON'T KNOW WHERE, DON'T KNOW WHEN,
BUT I KNOW YOU'LL HEAR THIS SONG
AGAIN...
AND AGAIN...

Very soon she was being called 'The Forces Sweetheart'. Something about the sad, yearning quality of her voice reminded every soldier, sailor and airman of the girl he'd left behind. So too did the songs she sang. 'We'll Meet Again', 'Yours' and 'White Cliffs of Dover'. Her greatest success was a German song called 'Lily Marlene' which Monty's Eighth Army had picked up in Africa. They claimed to have captured it from the Germans!

Vera Lynn entertained the troops with concerts, tours and radio broadcasts throughout the war. She sang again not long ago, as part of the recent D-Day anniversary celebrations. It's nice to think that one British institution is still with us...

INDEX